Reclaimed

Reclaimed

Faith in an Emerging Generation

DENISE JANSSEN

Foreword by Margaret Ann Crain

JUDSON PRESS
PUBLISHERS SINCE 1824

Join our mailing list for updates and special offers.
www.judsonpress.com/mailing_list.cfm

Reclaimed: Faith in an Emerging Generation
© 2015 by Denise Janssen
All rights reserved.

Judson Press has made every effort to trace the ownership of all quotes. In the event of a question arising from the use of a quote, we regret any error made and will be pleased to make the necessary correction in future printings and editions of this book.

Unless otherwise indicated, Bible quotations in this volume are from the New Revised Standard Version of the Bible, copyright 1989 by the Division of Christian Education of the National Council of the Churches of Christ in the U.S.A. Used by permission. All rights reserved.

Interior and cover design by Wendy Ronga/Hampton Design Group

Library of Congress Cataloging-in-Publication data
Janssen, Denise.
Reclaimed : faith in an emerging generation / Denise Janssen. — first [edition]. pages cm
ISBN 978-0-8170-1765-1 (pbk.: alk. paper) 1. Young adults—Religious life. I. Title.
BV4529.2.J37 2015
277.3'0830842—dc23   2015004051

Printed in the U.S.A.
First printing, 2015.

CONTENTS

FOREWORD

Every leader of a mainline Protestant congregation in the United States, lay or clergy, will immediately recognize the situation that Dr. Denise Janssen identifies in *Reclaimed*. We have walked alongside youth whose faith is heartfelt and strong. We have heard their passionate desire to make the world a better place. And then we have watched those young people disappear from the church as they move into young adulthood. We love these young people, and we grieve that they are absent from our congregations.

Statistics confirm that the millennial generation is missing from our churches. We who care about the future of the church are fearful as we consider what this missing generation may signal. We do not know what to do. Fortunately, Denise Janssen has offered both theoretical and concrete help in this volume. Those who are pastors, youth leaders, evangelists, church leaders, parents, grandparents, educators, and anyone else who loves a young adult and also loves the church will find this book a compelling read.

Reclaimed is a practical theology; it brings together the best wisdom from both social science and theology to analyze the current realities of young adults in North American and of the Protestant mainline churches. Janssen also shares her own research, which involved deep listening to the young adults whose stories are shared in this volume. The result is a vision for reclaiming the missing generation and the promise they offer.

First of all, this compelling vision reminds us that chronological age does not ensure "grown-up" qualities. Becoming a grown-up comes to humans all in good time, not when we reach a certain chronological age. The work of young adults involves grappling with the choices of vocation and identity. As we read the stories of the young adults that Janssen shares, we see grown-up humans emerging. These grown-up people are faithful and committed to a vocation that cooperates in the *missio Dei*. Their leadership will bring the church to new vitality and authentic mission. We need these young adults!

Second, the rich stories from real young adults will rekindle hope and love in anyone who was slipping toward a cynical view of their generation. Over and over in these stories, Janssen introduces young adults who care about the environment, about vulnerable people, about justice and compassion. The stories draw us through the volume, making it both entertaining and insightful. Janssen helps us see that even when young adults are missing from our congregations, many of them may be engaged in a "faithful fallow" period that will allow them to return to the life of the congregation ready to participate and lead. Janssen has recast our understanding of their absence into a positive light. And she presents portraits of young men and women whose period of faithful fallowness does not signal a loss of faith. Rather it is a time for individuation and discernment.

Third, through the stories of these young adults, we learn how to shape youth ministries that provide the authenticity to bring young adults into active presence in the church when they emerge into adulthood. Some of what we thought was effective youth ministry is not sufficient to bring young people back to church. The insights gained from Janssen's interviews provide critical clues to youth ministry that succeeds in forming adult disciples.

Finally, Janssen offers concrete advice to congregations seeking to welcome and include young adults in their life together. She doesn't shrink from reminding us that some of us will need to step aside and make space for the new generation. Such welcome and inclusion are less about getting the perfect program and more about welcoming the gifts of the Spirit they will bring in their faith. Janssen writes, "Adolescents (and young adults) are searching for something *to live for*, to give meaning to their lives and engage their passions. They are looking for that which will make their lives worth living, for that thing that is worth the investment of themselves." Cleaning up after the fellowship supper is probably not worth the investment of themselves, for instance. Yet, through Janssen's research we meet young adults in whose hands the church will thrive and faithfulness will increase.

This book rings with authenticity and compassion. That is due to Janssen's many years of experience in camping and youth ministry. She has served as a pastor. She has also worked in development. And she is currently teaching in a seminary. She brings her deep engagement with youth and the church to help all of us to understand the young adults in this story.

This book will encourage, focus, and open the church to the possibilities presented by a generation of young adults ready to lead the church.

Margaret Ann Crain

Professor Emeritus of Christian Education

Garrett-Evangelical Theological Seminary

PREFACE

"Where Have All the Flowers Gone?"[1]
A Study Born Out of Love for Those Missing from the Family of Faith

The journey that led to the creation of this book was a deeply emotional one for me. For many years, from 1987 to 2006, I served as a professional in the field of youth ministry. Although it was my job, ministry with youth was so much more than that. I worked in local congregations, at camps, and at the judicatory and denominational level. I still do, though my work is much broader these days. During those years, I encountered hundreds of passionate adolescents who loved God and earnestly sought to live into the emerging vocations to which they understood God was calling them. I was privileged to be a companion on their journey, with some for just a little while, and with others for a while longer. In the time we journeyed together, we had many deep conversations about the meaning of life. We worked countless hours in local social justice ministries and on summer mission trips, sweating for the love of those we served. We planned worship services together, and many youth found their voices and told their stories in words, music, slides, and actions. We laughed together and played together. We asked questions and tried to make sense of the journey of faith together. I saw in these youth the emerging shoots of the grown-up flowers they were becoming, full of grace and hope.

In most cases, they moved on to colleges far away, and I followed their continuing journeys with great interest, although often from afar. In every case where they would permit it, I would offer introductions to colleagues in the area and congregations with which they could connect. Sometimes the distractions of college life or the allure of new freedoms got in the way of connecting with a congregation during college. More often, sometimes years later, I heard from these grown-up youth that they had become agnostic, hardened against the possibility that the God of their youth even existed. But these were youth whose lives I had shared deeply for a time. I had heard them give voice to their faith commitments. I had heard them and watched them live their faith in prophetic ways. I could not help my skepticism—my suspicion that their professed agnosticism was a cover. My deepest hunches, or maybe fears, told me something went wrong during their adolescent years or after, something that kept them from living as faithful disciples of Jesus in the grown-up world in the ways I had observed during their adolescence. A desire to create more effective youth ministry that better prepared adolescents for the transition to adulthood was the first impetus for this study. In the words of Pete Seeger, "Where have all the flowers gone?" I asked with deep sadness about those emerging adults. And "Why have they gone?"

I had some hunches about the problem I had identified when I began this research, driven first to a doctoral program to gain new tools to address my questions more effectively. I was introduced to the tools of qualitative research and saw the benefits of understanding a small number of research participants and their experiences in great depth. I identified ethnography as a particularly useful research method in addressing my questions, believing the best way to understand what brings emerging and young adults into active relationship with a congregation is to ask them. Ethnography seeks narratives with thick, rich descriptions of the lived experiences of real people as a foundation from which to glean insights. It seemed useful to talk with those most likely to be involved in a congregation—young adults who had already been invested in a congregation in their adolescence. And it seemed best to explore further the experience of those who found their way into active engagement in congregations as young adults; in short, to interview those who had experienced a different or an atypical outcome. That's what my research sought to accomplish.

Before the Study: How I Conceived This Research

The project I proposed was a qualitative study of young adults who were involved in congregations as adolescents in the upper Midwest. I interviewed young adults for whom church was once important enough to get them actively involved, and either still is or has become important once again. Through our conversations, I hoped to understand why they were currently involved in congregations, and what their faith meant to them as adolescents and what it means to them presently. I also hoped to explore the role their congregation and its youth ministry played when they were adolescents, and the role other youth or adults in their congregation played in their lives then and now. Through colleagues, I had access to a few young adults who attended church-related camps when they were adolescents, at which I was a counselor. These weren't people with whom I had deep ongoing friendships, but I knew something of their faith, at least as they presented themselves at camp. Beginning with these contacts, I used a snowball method to identify additional potential interview candidates.

I envisioned unstructured interviews with these young adults to better understand the reasons for their investment in a congregation. I was interested in hearing from interview participants about the ways in which their own congregations and youth ministry programs (most of them in mainline Protestant congregations) failed or were faithful in forming disciples among adolescents. I was curious about the ways in which they understood their own mainline Protestant congregations were taking seriously (or failing to) the developmental stages and needs of adolescents and young adults in their disciple-forming activities. I was intrigued about study participants' perspectives on the ways in which a congregation's stated theology, as well as its implicit and null theologies,[2] helped or hindered its work of forming faithful disciples among adolescents.

I also had questions about the resilience of the research participants to find places of active engagement in their congregations. From anecdotal information about some potential research participants' experiences, I knew that in more than one case, congregations had been anything but hospitable to them. Still, they persisted in claiming their voices and their places in these congregations or in others. On the whole, I hadn't experienced these potential research participants as having personal or social issues such that they somehow sought to be treated badly or punitively. This made me ask questions about what made them more resilient than others in persisting with active congregational involvement. What made them different?

All of these questions ultimately took me back to questions about the congregations themselves. It seemed that based on the insights gained through this study, there would be something helpful for congregations to learn about welcoming young adults into their communities of faith, as well as something helpful to learn about the core values of youth ministry and the transition from adolescence through emerging adulthood to young adulthood. Like Pete Seeger, I wonder when we will learn, when we will acknowledge our shortsightedness and assumptions. As a Christian educator who deeply values learning, I hoped most of all to learn something personally and for the benefit of congregations like those I had served.

Initial Observations

My intent with this research was to interview young adults, continuing to listen to their experiences until I began to hear redundancy. I found redundancy before I completed twenty interviews. When I began this project, I believed the results of this research would contribute something important to the church's understanding of these critical years. As an educator, my intent was that the church and youth ministry practitioners might learn something about where all the "flowers" have gone—the young women and young men of Pete Seeger's song—and why. The church needs their gifts and their passion, and their loss from its midst is palpable. Now having completed the study and reflecting back on it, I believe even more strongly that the insights it offers bring with them an opportunity to break the cycle and learn from the experiences shared by these young adults.

This project would simply be a neat academic exercise, producing results that are both interesting and useful, if it were not for the fact that I am personally invested in it. The young adults I interviewed and the young adults who are "grown-up youth" from youth groups I pastored are real people to me. I care deeply about this issue—the absence of young adults from congregations—and it is because I care deeply about these people. I was driven to do this study in part because of my love for them and so many others like them.

I was driven to do this study out of a sense that an injustice was taking place about which I could do something. According to the findings of this research, the church serves young adults well when it invites them into real relationships with people of all ages, gives them opportunities to use their gifts to serve others, and gives them space to work things out in their own time while maintaining the connection that caring friends have when one is struggling. And the church does not serve young adults well when it fails to live up to its own call to love God with everything it has and is, and to love neighbor as self.

This is not just research to me. It is personal. I am talking about people I love here. My faith demands that I use my voice to help their voices be heard.

Notes

1. Pete Seeger, "Where Have All the Flowers Gone?" Fall River Music, 1961.

2. Here I refer to the idea that a congregation has a set of ideas and values that it teaches explicitly, but that sometimes competing ideas and values are taught implicitly by the way the congregation behaves as well as by what it chooses to leave out or not talk about (null). See Maria Harris, *Fashion Me a People: Curriculum in the Church* (Louisville: Westminster John Knox, 1989), 68–70.

INTRODUCTION

Bethany was stunned. Back in worship at the "Christmas-and-Easter-and-when-my-parents-visit" church of her twenties, she found herself dumb-struck at the way she had just been treated. She had been engaged in worship on this Sunday when she attended on her own, sensing that she just needed some peace and the church had at least been good for that. The pastor, a fortysomething woman, invited the congregation to join her in reading the Scripture text for the day, projected on the screen. Bethany found the Scripture intriguing and wanted to read it again for herself, perhaps in another translation. She had just called up the Scripture on her phone to have another look when the woman in front of her turned around and chastised her loudly enough for everyone around to hear. "That's just disrespectful!" the woman, whom she didn't know, admonished, assuming Bethany was "just messing around" on her phone rather than paying attention.

* * *

When Bryan started attending the quaint little church near his new home, he and his wife were drawn to the way in which the congregation celebrated their two young children, creating personalized programs just for them. They were among just two or three families their age in a congregation averaging about seventy years old. The church building was older and smelled musty, but the people were friendly and it began to feel like home. Older members had been discussing the discomfort they were feeling sitting on the hardwood pews. It made perfect sense to Bryan, since the congregation also needed more space, that they remove the pews and bring in padded chairs, which would increase the comfort and make the worship space more modular. Discussion ensued and folks seemed open, but the idea was dismissed without a vote at a business meeting. Instead, the congregation voted to pad the pews (at an exorbitant rate). An older member was overheard saying, "We just like our pews. If the younger folks want chairs, let them vote for that in ten years after we're gone." Sadly, the younger adults won't be around then either.

Every Christian denomination today finds itself wondering, *Where have all the young adults gone? Why don't they come to church?* Merely observing the ages of those present in a typical mainline Protestant worship service affirms the reality that young adults are present in worship and active in congregations at a far lower percentage of the congregation than most other adult age groups. Their rate of participation is far lower than the percentage of people in their age range in the general population. If we look deeper for emerging and young adults active in leadership in congregations, we find even fewer.

Speculation abounds regarding the reasons for this observed phenomenon, but it more often takes the form of judgment and blaming; for example, "If the park district wouldn't schedule soccer on Sundays, those young families would be in church." Many middle and older adults remember becoming involved with a congregation as young adults with their children, and that there were many other young adults involved alongside them. "So what's with this current generation?" they ask. "Why aren't they coming to church?" Quietly among themselves, older members often ask a far more practical question about where the energetic, able-bodied members will come from who will take over from them the work in the church that they have continued doing far past their interest and physical ability to do it. Some fear their church will die.

We can make inferences about how congregations diagnose the "problem" from the attempts they make to address it. One way congregations hope to attract young adults is with "contemporary worship"— essentially the same traditional worship service repackaged with praise and worship music from the 1970s and '80s played on acoustic guitars and keyboards. Coffee bars and casual dress, as well as projected lyrics and "relevant" preaching attempt to draw young adults. Parenting programs, including "mother's day out" –style programs, attempt to do the same. Worship services at alternative times and in alternative locations were a popular strategy for a while. These strategies, while well-intentioned, have mostly missed the mark, sometimes attracting older baby boomers but not the current young adult generation.

All of these strategies—and dozens more like them—have failed far more often than they have succeeded, evidenced by the ongoing absence of young adults from congregational life. I believe they failed, in part, because each incorrectly assumed a reason for the absence of the young adults they were trying to attract. Such strategies attempt to replace relationships with programming and packaging. Clearly, this is a complicated issue.

Do an online search and you'll find an extensive list of books that try to get at this issue of young adults' absence from congregations. Clearly this matter concerns someone. Congregations are advised in many of these books, though there are some notable exceptions,[1] to attract young adults with cosmetic adjustments and superficial program changes targeting young adults. All this programming is urged when what those young adults most need is what all of us need: real relationships with people across the age spectrum, opportunities to encounter the holy, and a chance to partner with others to use their gifts to make a difference for good in this world. The injustice in the way churches are advised to attract people is that they end up treating those people as if they are not the strong, compassionate, and intelligent people I know from my interviews and from my youth groups. The greatest injustice is inflicted when churches fail to treat them as real grown-up humans and involve them in the church's life, preferring instead to decide for them what they need or want and then program at them.

In the course of ministry over the last few years, I heard anecdotal remarks about church experiences again and again from young adults I encountered, young adults such as Bethany and Bryan and many more. Maybe because they know I'm a pastor, the children of congregants asking me to perform their weddings or former youth from past ministry settings share their church stories, both positive and negative. Their stories don't all end with them happily engaged in lives of faith supported by faith communities. What these anecdotal conversations indicated to me as I began to consider this project was that there was at least the potential to learn something important by listening carefully and deeply to the particular experiences of particular young adults. In the anecdotes, I heard about important people in these young adults' lives. I saw young adults whose faith drove them to keep searching for a "big enough God"[2] when the God they were offered at church was more limited than their experience indicated. I saw people in each of their lives who took seriously their questions. I observed congregations that helped them figure out who they were in the world—their Christian vocation. And I heard a lot of stories about the way congregations and congregants behaved that made me ask, with Pete Seeger, when we in congregations will ever learn, when we will begin to pay attention.

Simplistic answers to these complicated issues have fallen short. This book seeks to offer a sustained look at faith in the context of the real lives of actual people: the young adults I interviewed. It is an invitation to the reader to enter into these young adults' life stories and find the beauty and the struggle and the very real faith that is passionately present there. And it is a challenge and a call to those of us who have been in the pews a while longer to understand the deep and abiding love of God that may be present in ways we aren't looking for. As we seek to understand the faith *of* this emerging generation, my hope is that your faith *in* this emerging generation will grow, as well.

Notes

1. Judson Press has released a variety of titles in recent years approaching these questions from various angles. Such books include Ralph C. Watkins with Jason A. Barr Jr., Jamal Bryant, William H. Curtis, and Otis Moss III, *The Gospel Remix: Reaching the Hip Hop Generation* (2007); Russell Rathbun, *nuChristian: Finding Faith in a New Generation* (2009); Benjamin Stephens and Ralph C. Watkins, *From Jay-Z to Jesus:*

Reaching and Teaching Young Adults in the Black Church (2009); Jolene Erlacher, ed., *Millennials in Ministry* (2014); Kathryn Mary Lohre, *For Such a Time as This: Young Adults on the Future of the Church* (2014); and Adam L. Bond and Laura Mariko Cheifetz, eds., *Church on Purpose: Reinventing Discipleship, Community, & Justice* (2015).

2. I draw here on a metaphor about big enough questions from Sharon Daloz Parks, *Big Questions, Worthy Dreams: Mentoring Young Adults in Their Search for Meaning, Purpose, and Faith* (San Francisco: Jossey-Bass, 2000), 165–66.

PART ONE

PREPARING THE WAY

For teenager Sierra, singing was the most fun she ever had. Every time she sang on Youth Sunday, the congregation celebrated her gifts and praised her beautiful voice and her poised delivery. She had the opportunity to take voice lessons, and she found herself desiring to sing something more challenging. Her voice teacher assured her that she should have no problem singing the repertoire with the adults' sanctuary choir. Sierra approached the choir director one Sunday and asked about singing with the adults, enthusiastically sharing her voice teacher's endorsement. She felt like a door was slammed in her face when the choir director emphatically declared that no children were permitted in the adult choir, period. She needed to wait her turn.

* * *

Nick, a young adult, had just joined the church council as an at-large member after having been part of the congregation for a number of years. At one council meeting, the task force planning the annual block party made its report, asserting their goal of involving every group in the congregation to help with the outreach event. Nick started to think through the young adults he could recruit: Adam had his own food cart business; Grayland could provide music as a DJ; Leticia could create publicity materials and sidewalk art. When Nick raised his hand to suggest contacting these friends to share their gifts, a task force member said she was glad Nick was volunteering—and would the young adults please set up and clean up since they were young and strong enough to do it?

Nick and his friends did what they were asked but were not really invested in the event. The block party was carried out by the same people doing the same things in the same old way. Instead of reaching hundreds from the community, Nick and his friends cleaned up after event that brought in a couple dozen people.

1

The Faith Lives of Young Adults

You don't have to be very smart to be an adult; some people prove it to you. They get promoted every year on their birthday when they ought to be held back because they still have work to do. —Garrison Keillor

Noted author Sharon Parks uses the Garrison Keillor quote above to illustrate an important point in her book *Big Questions, Worthy Dreams*: being an adult in a chronological way does not necessarily translate into adult actions or responses.[1] Human development seems to happen at its own pace in a curiously nonlinear fashion whether you're 25 or 52. Nowhere is this truer than in the case of emerging and young adults who are chronologically adults even though they may be working on the developmental tasks of adolescence, emerging adulthood, and young adulthood for a number of years—even revisiting them again later in life.

To provide some ideas for considering this transition to adulthood through a new set of lenses, Parks suggests:

> Adulthood is a way of making meaning. To be an adult is:
>   1. to be aware of one's own composing of reality,
>   2. to participate self-consciously in an ongoing dialogue toward truth, and
>   3. to be able to sustain a capacity to respond—to take responsibility for seeing and reweaving (in activity of one's every day) a fitting pattern of relationships between the disparate elements of self and world.[2]

In this way of understanding adulthood, faith is a set of lenses through which we perceive meaning in our lives. Indeed, faith serves as a filter that allows us to compose meaning for ourselves. Throughout our lives, our meaning-making work becomes ever more encompassing and unifying. Understood in this way, we can see that faith isn't just something Christians or other religious people do; rather, faith as making meaning is something all people do. When we make meaning together in similar ways, we are practicing a religion.[3]

Young adults develop at their own pace and become involved in their own meaning-making activities, which naturally include faith issues. What young adults need most during this developmental place in their lives are safe spaces and people with whom to explore meaning in their lives and in the world. The primary role of the faith community in ministry with emerging and young adults is to be hospitable to "big questions" about the complex mystery of life.

Most mainline faith communities would affirm this idea that young adults are in the process of wrestling with life's big questions. Those mainline churches would say they welcome big questions in their faith community, probably contrasting themselves with those *other* churches who would "tell you what you had to believe" or "get all tied up in dogma." Yet the pews in most progressive mainline churches are as empty of young adults as any other segment of the Christian church. There may be some youth present, but congregations with many young adults in attendance are the exception rather than the norm.

It is this complicated and evolving period of transition from adolescence through emerging adulthood and into young adulthood—and, in particular, the meaning-making or faith aspects of this transition—that create the space and material for this research. In asking the question "What experiences from adolescence make it more likely for a young adult to be actively engaged in a faith community?" I mean to hold up a mirror to local congregations. We can gain new insights by listening deeply to the life stories of a group of faithful young adults who are living out their Christian vocations in and through the local church. In hearing about their experiences and reflecting on how they made meaning of those experiences, I hope to offer some food for thought to local churches as they seek to understand something of the faith lives of young adults in their midst.

Emerging Adulthood, Young Adulthood, and the Church

Sociologist Jeffrey Jensen Arnett explores the transition from adolescence to young adulthood in a book titled *Emerging Adulthood: The Winding Road from the Late Teens through the Twenties*.[4] He sees significant changes over the last sixty-five years in the way young adults develop—significant enough to identify a new developmental period, "emerging adulthood." I concur that the playing field has changed and people develop differently today in adolescence and young adulthood than they did in the middle of the last century.[5] While Sharon Parks argues for the period called young adulthood as a distinct phase of development, Arnett further divides the period into emerging adulthood and young adulthood—each with distinct characteristics.

Arnett understands emerging adulthood to be a time of exploring identity through one's relationships and work. Most emerging adults have plenty of exposure to both rewarding and painful relationships in their families of origin and, although relationships with parents may change substantially during emerging adulthood, parents are still very important. "Serial monogamy" perhaps best describes the growing trend in typical peer love relationships in adolescence and emerging adulthood. Although most emerging adults intend to marry "someday," many seem to imagine that day to be years away. Trying out different kinds of partners through a series of relationships seems to be the new "courting."

The kinds of explorations young adults undertake in career and relationships bring with them instability. Trying out various types of work and relationships in this way can make emerging adults seem self-absorbed or self-indulgent, or at least self-focused. The reality is that opportunities to try out various ways of making meaning in relationships, commitments, and vocations are vital to the work of learning how to compose meaning for themselves during this period of life. Work may well be a means of self-expression during this period. This is an important shift in the way human development takes place (or is expected to take place) compared to the process of fifty to seventy-five years ago. What is understood by some to be a means of supporting oneself (work, vocation) is loaded with all the meaning-making freight that was reserved in previous generations for family (or even religion). For those for whom adulthood meant getting a job, getting married, and having a family in one's late teens or early twenties, it may very well seem unclear when a person who is legally adult should be regarded as an adult culturally.

Emerging adults feel "in between" and, in many ways, they are. The markers that once seemed to clearly define transitions between periods of human development are no longer the definite and clear rites of passage they once were. There is a "both-and" quality to emerging adulthood that can feel duplicitous both for the emerging adults and for other generations. The meaning each makes of the same event or circumstance is simply different. Let's face it: it's confusing when, for example, college students have a right to privacy with regard to their grades—privacy even from their parents who may be paying for their college education. Parks describes this as being self-determining without quite being self-sufficient. At the same time, the glory of emerging adulthood that perhaps wasn't a part of prior generations' experience is, to use Arnett's words, the "unvanquished hope" that is possible about one's ability to positively impact our world. For those in previous generations who felt forced into a career that was little more than a job to support a family, this kind of freedom to explore vocation and meaning in life can seem foreign—and wonderful at the same time.

Faith in Emerging and Young Adulthood

To set the stage for the place of faith in emerging and young adulthood, we turn first to research into the faith lives of adolescents. A major national study of youth and religion, detailed in the book *Soul Searching*, found that 44 percent of mainline Protestant teens attend church weekly and another 16 percent attend religious services two to three times a month. The study indicates they would attend more often if it was entirely up to them: 47 percent would attend weekly and 20 percent would participate two to three times a month. What the study indicates, based on these percentages, is that more than half of mainline Protestant teens are in church more than half the time.

At the same time, this study observed that while adolescents may intend to be more involved in congregations, they are incredibly inarticulate about what they believe. Overall, teens seem to believe in a Creator God who gives order to the world and watches over humans. That God wants people to be nice to each other, be happy, and have good self-esteem. God doesn't necessarily get involved in the everyday lives of most people except as a problem solver. In addition, all good people go to heaven when they die. But this set of beliefs (dubbed "moralistic therapeutic deism" by the researchers) is largely a tacit creed of many teens, who seem unable or disinclined to articulate such beliefs in a more formal or orthodox way.[6]

In the face of these findings, I wonder: *How are youth formed by the worship services they attend, however often they attend them? What is the content of the faith they claim, and how does it affect them?* Faith may be contagious, but it cannot be "caught" through the air; human contact is required for it to be transmitted. Just "attending" doesn't do it. The good news of God's love and grace must seep inside and transform the person attending. Failing that, the impact of attending church services is slight.

So, while half of mainline Protestant teens surveyed in this study said faith was very or extremely important, and while 55 percent reported being involved in a youth group, they don't seem to be getting much help from the churches they attend in knowing how to express or live out the faith they say is so important to them. The absence of young adults from communities of faith raises real questions about the adequacy of the God about whom the church is teaching.[7]

One emerging adult described the challenge to her faith that came during a college class in theology when her eyes were opened to the critical academic study of religion instead of the more devotional and dogmatic faith she was taught in church: "I'm going, 'Wait a minute. These Catholics have lied to me my whole life.'"[8] This response and others like it make me wonder about the content and quality of the religious education these emerging adults received as children and youth. The young female study participant's response makes me wonder: *If we could hear about the faith this emerging adult respondent is rejecting, perhaps we would affirm that we don't believe in that God either.*

Arnett identifies the emerging adult urge to make decisions for themselves as another reason for the minimal role of congregations in the faith lives of emerging adults. "[T]o accept what their parents have taught them about religion and carry on the same religious traditions as their parents would represent a kind of failure, an abdication of their responsibility to think for themselves, become independent from their parents, and decide on their own beliefs."[9] Arnett observes from survey and interview responses that this "rugged individualism" softens when emerging adults become parents—it seems they are more likely to be motivated by their children than their parents to adopt a religious tradition and practice within it. Thus, creating safe and hospitable space for exploration of life's big questions seems critical to the faith transition from childhood, through adolescence, and into adulthood.

Is the church's failure to provide such space for the big questions in adolescence the reason we aren't seeing young adults in church? Barna research suggests that faith is still important to young adults: 80 percent say faith is very important, three-quarters claim to have prayed in the last week, and nearly 60 percent claim to have made a personal commitment to Jesus. They just don't attend church regularly: only 30 percent say they've attended church in the last week—the same percentage as have donated anything to a church in the last year or read the Bible in the last week.[10] These findings aren't limited to one end or the other of the theological spectrum.[11]

These insights lead us to ask about the role of the church in the lives of young adults. In what ways can the church better attend to the uniqueness of faith development in the emerging and young adult periods of life? How can the church better pay attention to the transition from childhood through adolescence into adulthood?

Scholars who are writing about emerging and young adults in the church shed light on important aspects of congregational life that aid young adults in or impede them from becoming actively involved in congregations. Carol Howard Merritt's work *Tribal Church: Ministering to the Missing Generation* is particularly helpful in illustrating that a congregation's own health (or lack thereof) contributes to the likelihood of young adults becoming involved in and feeling comfortable in and connected to that congregation. In her book Merritt describes the ageist way in which people in their twenties and thirties are treated by congregations, and the way in which this replicates the culture (where baby boomers hold on to power and anyone under forty or fifty is assumed to be too young to have a valid opinion or the ability to act responsibly).

Merritt goes on to describe the circle of relationships to which people in this nomadic emerging adult subculture relate as a tribe, and further advocates for this understanding of a congregation: a tribal church. In using the term "tribal church," Merritt means a group of people who gather around a common cause, recognizing that most young adults' ministry need is first to secure basic care, to share the practice of religious traditions (both historic and emerging traditions, not "the way we've always done it"), and to find encouragement in an intergenerational network in the congregation.[12]

While Merritt's work helps us to make sense of those emerging and young adults who find their way to meaningful ministry within healthy congregations, it still seems there is a disconnect between adolescence and young adulthood in terms of active engagement of the majority of these young people in the life of a congregation. This disconnect is substantial and compelled me to do my own ethnographic research. Ethnography, with its thick and rich narratives shared by the emerging and young adults we are trying to understand, offers our best hope for learning how to companion them on their life and faith journeys. In the section "A Way Back Home," what I heard from those young adults will help us to take seriously the actual lived experiences of a few emerging and young adults as a window to understanding and changing our habits. Next, let's take a look at the state of youth ministry as the context of the faith grounding many young adults bring with them into young adulthood.

Notes

1. Sharon Daloz Parks, *Big Questions, Worthy Dreams: Mentoring Young Adults in Their Search for Meaning, Purpose, and Faith* (San Francisco: Jossey-Bass, 2000), 37–38.

2. Sharon Parks, *The Critical Years: The Young Adult Search for a Faith to Live By* (New York: Harper & Row, 1986), 6.

3. Parks, *Big Questions, Worthy Dreams*, 197.

4. Jeffrey Jensen Arnett, *Emerging Adulthood: The Winding Road from the Late Teens through the Twenties* (New York: Oxford University Press, 2004).

5. For further information, see Erik Erikson, *Identity: Youth and Crisis* (New York: W. W. Norton, 1968); L. S. Vygotsky, *Mind in Society: The Development of Higher Psychological Processes* (Cambridge, MA: Harvard University Press, 1978); Parks, *The Critical Years*.

6. Christian Smith and Melissa Lundquist Denton, *Soul Searching: The Religious and Spiritual Lives of American Teenagers* (New York: Oxford University Press, 2005).

7. Ibid., 166.

8. Arnett, *Emerging Adulthood*, 176.

9. Ibid., 177.

10. Kristen Campbell, "Young Adults Missing from Pews," *Christian Century* 121, no. 3 (February 10, 2004): 16.

11. For a more evangelical perspective, see Dan Kimball, *They Like Jesus but Not the Church: Insights from Emerging Generations* (Grand Rapids: Zondervan, 2007).

12. Carol Howard Merritt, *Tribal Church: Ministering to the Missing Generation* (Herndon, VA: Alban Institute, 2008), 6–9.

2

Adolescence in the Church
Youth Ministry's Role in
Shaping Young Adult Faith

Youth ministry is the context in which the faith lives of many adolescents are fostered in the church. Whatever the cause, it seems undisputed that the transition from adolescence to young adulthood in mainline Protestant faith traditions is far from seamless. Scholars posit a variety of theories about the disconnect between the faith lives of adolescents and those of emerging and young adults. In this chapter, we'll consider some of the gaps in the faith transition.

Passion in Search of a Worthy Cause

Once upon a time, when churchgoing was far more common at all ages, the Protestant church experienced a kind of continental drift that historians describe as the fundamentalist-modernist conflict. Kenda Creasy Dean has characterized it as a controversy between "being good" versus "doing good." The debate ultimately created a divide among Protestants, with the evangelical church emphasizing "being good" while the mainline church emphasized "doing good" (also known as the social gospel movement).

Fast-forward to the twenty-first century, and Dean (a mainline Protestant teaching at a mainline Protestant institution) observes that the mainline church fails to connect its emphasis on doing good with a passionate love of God and neighbor that drives the doing. It no longer offers adolescents a passionate cause to connect with their developmental need for one. The kind of fervor often associated with evangelicalism as a passion for "saving lost souls" provides a clue to what is missing in the more intellectual pursuits of justice: the kind of passion that adolescents need from faith—something "to die for."[1] The solution, according to Dean, boils down to helping adolescents see how the passion of Christ connects with their own passions, giving them a faith "to die for." I am not content with Dean's implication, using this clever metaphor, that adolescents ultimately have "death" in mind. Rather, I would cast it in this way: adolescents (and young adults) are searching for something *to live for*, to give meaning to their lives and engage their passions. They are looking for that which will make their lives worth living, for that thing that is worth the investment of themselves.

If we need an illustration of how such passion in search of a cause can be tapped, we need look no further than the droves of young adults who became engaged in Barack Obama's presidential campaign in 2008, who participated in the demonstrations that were part of the Occupy movement of the late 2000s, and who turned out in 2014 to protest police killings of unarmed black men.

This kind of activism is not a new phenomenon with this generation—consider the crowds of young adults who marched for civil and voting rights, campaigned for Eugene McCarthy, protested the Vietnam War, and flocked to folk masses with guitars in hand after Vatican II. This sort of passion doesn't wait for committees or planning meetings, so a conserving organization like the church often finds it difficult to capitalize on its energy and enthusiasm. This fervor to do good is typically out front of planning structures and well-ordered processes for approval. The movement of the Spirit rarely complies with the competing need for structure and rules.

One of the best strategies for churches who are out of practice with engaging adolescent and young adult passion is to pay attention and observe places where their passion is already being engaged and then join in where there is a missional fit. For example, when young adults in a neighborhood are organizing to create composting sites or community gardens or collecting signatures to press the political structures to develop low-cost options for purchasing fresh food in a struggling neighborhood, the church can join in with those efforts already in progress. How many churches have more lawn than they know what to do with and could provide space to grow vegetables to feed hungry neighbors? When ownership of the idea is not required and ulterior motives (such as adding members and increasing giving) are removed from the equation, the church is free to live out its mission in tangible ways. Middle and older adults are reenergized by the passion and energy of young adults working alongside them.

Flipping the Script for Success

An important gift the church has to offer emerging and young adults exists in the alternate scripts our faith provides for a successful—or better yet, meaningful—life. Adolescents and emerging adults, being hyper aware of the broken places they observe in adult life, frequently attempt to redefine a successful or meaningful life on their own terms. Being unwilling to punch their predecessors' time clocks, they long for alternate definitions and pathways as they anticipate constructing meaningful lives in adulthood. Let's explore an example of this.

Scholar and author Brian Mahan tells of a day in a university class he taught on the ethics of ambition when he introduced a story about a college senior he met who turned down admission to Yale Law School to serve in the Peace Corps for a year. The students in his class spent the next three sessions completely absorbed with the ethical dilemma this raised for them—clearly it touched a very tender spot deep inside them.[2] Informed by the culture's drive for success, epitomized by acceptance into Yale Law School, these students suddenly found that the success script was in tension with the passion script that resonated so deeply with their emerging adult energy around injustice and making a difference, embodied by the Peace Corps option. Both options provide unique opportunities to do good, and choosing either, the students may have feared, would have lifelong consequences, closing some doors while opening others.

Why did this dilemma touch the students so deeply? Well, we know one of the foremost developmental tasks of adolescence and young adulthood is the formation of identity. At the time when adolescents and young adults are trying to develop that sense of identity, the primary cultural script tells them they need to "become something" through education, vocational training, employment, and the like. What we do and how well we're compensated for it is the standard way for adults to "size up" one another when we meet.

That is exactly what admission to Yale Law School would have represented—the opportunity to "be someone" and "do something important," as defined by society's norms of higher education and economic wealth. Yet the young woman's decision to enter the Peace Corps turns that definition of "importance" on its head. In fact, it has strong echoes of the gospel, which proclaims that "the last will be first, and the first will be last" (Matthew 20:16). Jesus, our primary Teacher, taught a different message of success.

So, when the message of our faith conflicts with the primary cultural script, the church needs to offer alternative scripts that help adolescents and young adults resolve the confusion and embrace the opportunity to live as faithful disciples. The implication for the church, particularly the mainline Protestant church, is that it needs to take seriously the notion of Christian vocation and connect with adolescents and young adults around that notion at a time in their lives when they need it most.

Because the scripts we're given by our culture can feel so overwhelmingly authoritative, youth in particular but people of faith of all ages need guidance and assistance as they seek to live lives of meaning and purpose. Going to work, raising children, interacting with neighbors—all these can become more meaningful and purposeful acts when we see them through the lenses of faith. Reflecting on the values our faith teaches and the ways those values can inform our actions and choices is something the church can teach and foster. Some congregations engage in mission trips or service projects as a focal point for youth to explore vocation. Others offer gifts inventories or offer assessments and tools to help youth clarify their gifts, interests, and passions. Exploring the intersection of our own passions and gifts with the great needs of the world around us is something in which the church specializes. Adolescents need this assistance, as do emerging and young adults—and frankly, so do the not-so-young adults in our congregations. Vocational exploration—not necessarily related to career choice—is a key place for the church to focus its energy. And some do, although often in a disjointed and episodic fashion.

What does a focus on vocation and call look like in practice? Again, paying attention plays a key role. Sustained conversation around these issues and a shared language for the dialogue are necessary. Further, this work of offering alternate scripts begs the question of the rest of the church: Have we in the church just accepted the culture's definition of success? We have more work to do if we have not engaged this question in the life of the congregation. That work will involve learning to question popularly held assumptions through the lenses of our faith, which implies we are wrestling with what we believe, why we believe it, and what it means for our lives. Becoming accustomed we believe it to new lenses when we get new glasses can take some time; likewise, learning to see our lives through the lenses of our faith may take some time, as well.

Alternate scripts are more "caught" than taught. When I see people choosing to live simply so they can give generously to others, I learn something implicitly even though nothing is taught explicitly. When my congregation gives positions to people based on their gifts and not their "stature" in the congregation, I learn something implicitly about priorities in the kingdom of God (which are different from those that dominate our culture). We may well find that the adolescents and young adults in our lives take the lead in identifying alternate scripts, placing the rest of the congregation in roles of support and encouragement as they seek to live them out.

More Substance, Less Sideshow

Most churches are familiar with youth ministry as an age-segregated and culturally dissonant ministry of the church. It meets at a time when more serious church groups won't be disturbed by the increased noise and activity levels of the adolescent participants. It centers on "fun and fellowship" more than on study or spiritual reflection or even mission and service. It strives to attract and entertain the teenagers more than it does to equip and empower them.

Such ministry efforts may be popular and seeker-friendly, but author David White asserts that this model of ministry disengages youth from the important work of discernment undertaken in the larger community of faith. Historically, discernment is the practice undertaken by the church when it seeks to resolve particular dilemmas in community and the world. We do it in business meetings and board or committee meetings, among other settings. Discernment often takes the shape of the visioning and missional planning we do in congregational life.

White seeks to expand the concept to become less episodic and more a way of life—across generations. He cites G. Stanley Hall, the first modern theorist of adolescence, who observed that this period of life was characterized by curiosity, passion, and aliveness.[3] The church does adolescents a disservice when we do not engage these qualities in helping them respond to the pain and joy of the world. Too much of youth ministry, White argues, is generic programming and hype—when what adolescents need are engagement and tools to use their natural energy and curiosity and vitality to cooperate with God's Spirit for the healing of the world.[4]

Because congregations are out of practice in taking seriously the gifts and insights of those who have not yet reached the cultural age of majority, which itself is a little slippery, this reengagement of adolescents and young adults in the congregation's discernment processes may need to take place in stages. Grown-ups will need time to shift their thinking regarding the value of the ideas and questions brought up by youth and young adults; they will need tools to help them listen and nurture those ideas as they emerge rather than squelch them. And those adolescents and young adults will need time to learn how to claim their gifts and their voices in the congregation among those who are older.

Groups often become easy marks for bullies, and congregations are groups much like any other, so this may be a time when congregational bullies need to be called out for their inappropriate behavior. Youth may need space and time with others in their own age group to practice discernment in a safer context. It is very difficult for groups of adults not to feel like they are "permitting" youth into adult conversations—youth who may themselves be full members of the congregation with all the rights and responsibilities that go along with full membership. Discerning the steps needed takes time and care and discipline and grace. How much more impactful might our ministry with adolescents transitioning to adulthood become if we as a congregation transitioned with them by intentionally engaging in discernment with them in new ways as they grow and change?

Behind the Numbers

The National Study of Youth and Religion offers some additional insight relating to adolescents, their engagement in religious services, and how such attendance affects them. For example, when asked about the importance of religious faith in shaping their daily lives, half of mainline Protestant adolescents surveyed reported that it was very important or extremely important.[5] And 55 percent reported that they were involved in a youth group in their church, while 49 percent said they were involved in their congregations.[6]

When pressed about what they believed, their religious practices, and the meaning of faith in their daily lives, however, most youth were described by the study's authors as being "incredibly inarticulate." This, combined with other factors, left researchers with the impression that religion is not all that important in their lives and that "teens are getting very little help from their religious communities in knowing how to express the faith that may be important to them."[7]

What Have We Learned?

Certainly it seems that mainline Protestant congregations have been doing a less-than-consistent job of helping adolescents know and experience the God they claim to believe in. As young adults, they don't seem to find attending church important to carry out and maintain the faith they have.

The national study does suggest that youth attend church and would do so more often if it were up to them. They seem ready to continue involvement in their current congregations and say that they believe doing so is good for them. But when they come to young adulthood, many do not continue to be involved in church.

This makes me wonder about the God the church is offering adolescents, what those adolescents believe (or don't believe) about that God, and what their faith has to do with the rest of their lives. It makes me speculate that part of the cause for that later disengagement is because our congregations also fail at times to help youth experience and know a sophisticated and complex God who can grow and change with them as they grow and change.

But while that may be part of the issue, I am convinced that the underlying issue goes back to the way in which the church too often fails to pay attention to what's important and stay focused on its God-given mission. Concern for budgets, buildings, programs, and keeping people happy becomes an end in itself sometimes and draws the church's attention away from fostering faith in the next generation or caring for those in need. The church can so easily become co-opted and distracted; faithfulness is hard work and requires focus and energy. If we focus on what's wrong, we become discouraged. So, rather than dwell on what's wrong, I'll offer an example of one congregation that seems to be getting it right. There are many more, but for now, let's focus on this one.

Dori Grinenko Baker's edited volume *Greenhouses of Hope* brought together a diverse group of voices lifting up examples of congregations who excel in particular ways of embracing the unique gifts and emerging voices of youth and young adults. In Baker's title image, quite literally "hothouses" where hope can grow for youth and young adults, we glimpse a vision of a different sort of role for a congregation: rather than "warehousing" youth and keeping them safe from the temptations of the world, a congregation might be an incubator to foster their growth. In order to function in this way, the congregation itself needs to be a hotbed of growth and nourishment that is alive with possibilities.

In a chapter of *Greenhouses* by Margaret Ann Crain titled "Staying Awake: When God Moments Echo in Community," a vocabulary and images that are both liberating and life-giving emerge to offer possibilities for congregations. Crain's chapter provides examples of an intergenerational fluidity of vocational exploration and conversation that fosters mutuality and space for the gifts of young people. Deeply impacted by their experiences with Appalachian Service Project, youth from the congregation gave leadership to groups of adults who were exposed to new ideas in their own service experiences. As both youth and adults explored their vocations in light of these new experiences, the congregation developed an intergenerational pattern and language around "God moments." As I reflected on the stories of participants from my own research (see the following chapters), these images brought into clearer focus the benefits and deficits I heard described in participants' own congregational experiences.[8]

Congregations can be a powerful space for youth and young adults to grow into an understanding of where their passions and gifts intersect with the opportunities and needs of our world. How do congregations discern what's important? The stories in the following chapters will help to inform this question.

Notes

1. Kenda Creasy Dean, *Practicing Passion: Youth and the Quest for a Passionate Church* (Grand Rapids: Eerdmans, 2004), 7.

2. Brian J. Mahan, *Forgetting Ourselves on Purpose: Vocation and the Ethics of Ambition* (San Francisco: Jossey-Bass, 2002), 1–8.

3. David F. White, *Practicing Discernment with Youth: A Transformative Youth Ministry Approach* (Cleveland: Pilgrim, 2005), 9.

4. Ibid., 5–10.

5. Christian Smith and Melissa Lundquist Denton, *Soul Searching: The Religious and Spiritual Lives of American Teenagers* (New York: Oxford University Press, 2005), table 7, 40.

6. Ibid., table 14, 51.

7. Ibid., 131.

8. Margaret Ann Crain, "Staying Awake," in Dori Grinenko Baker, ed., *Greenhouses of Hope: Congregations Growing Young Leaders Who Will Change the World* (Herndon, VA: Alban Institute, 2010), 2, 33–56.

3

The People behind the Stories— and the Statistics

Since we will spend some time in the coming chapters hearing the stories of participants from my study, please allow me to introduce them to you. Their names and other personal information has been changed or modified to protect their privacy.

When I embarked on this study, Tonya was the first potential participant I contacted. I remembered her from a camp she attended as an adolescent at which I served as a counselor. During her teen years, Tonya was insightful and genuine; she was a person who kept in touch with friends in between camp years, so I imagined she may still have contact with friends her age who might fit the qualifications of study participants, as well. Tonya consented to an interview and recruited several other study participants, as I hoped she might.

Tonya married a guy she dated at the camp where we met, and they live with their three children in her husband's hometown, just outside a large city in the Midwest. Tonya grew up in an old first church of a mainline denomination in a small midwestern river town. She attended the same college I had, starting the fall after I graduated, but she transferred after a year to be closer to her husband-to-be. She is very active in her children's lives and works part-time for an agency in a blighted neighborhood that serves at-risk adolescent girls in the city near their home. She and her husband attend a socially and theologically progressive new church start of the same denomination in which she grew up.

Morris is married to Tonya, and I knew him from camp too. He completed a degree in transportation management from the state university near his boyhood home and now leads a division of the transportation department at a major agribusiness corporation. As an adolescent, Morris attended with his family a medium-sized neighborhood congregation of a mainline denomination in a large midwestern city near where he grew up. Morris and Tonya met at church camp and married when they were nineteen and twenty-one, respectively. They were in their late thirties at the time of the study interviews.

Bill was in his early thirties at the time of this study. Morris and Tonya introduced him to me as a potential participant because he and they attend the same socially and theologically progressive new church start of a mainline denomination in that large midwestern city. Coincidentally, Bill attended the same medium-sized congregation as Morris for some of his adolescence; in fact, Morris and Tonya served as his youth group leaders for a time. He is a graduate student in an advanced professional degree program, having also attended a year of seminary. Bill is single and presently lives in a large midwestern city, having moved there a couple of years ago to go to graduate school.

Lisa is in her late thirties and works as a branch manager for a financial services firm in the suburban ring of a large midwestern city. She grew up in a county-seat town nearby where she attended an old downtown first church of a mainline denomination. Tonya suggested Lisa, whom we both knew from camp, for the study. Lisa attended a small, private liberal arts college, graduating with a degree in religious studies. As she came to understand herself as a lesbian, her relationship with the church wandered through some difficult times, but she found her way to an open and affirming mainline congregation in the large city where she lives, and she and her partner were married there five years ago.

Suzie also came to the study at the recommendation of Tonya; Suzie is Morris's sister and, thus, Tonya's sister-in-law. As with her brother Morris, Suzie grew up attending a medium-sized neighborhood congregation of a mainline denomination in a large midwestern city. Suzie attended a small, private liberal arts college but transferred after a year, graduating instead from a state school in her home state. She married her high school boyfriend a couple of years after college, and they live in that same small town where they grew up. For a number of years after they married, when they were starting their family, Suzie and her husband attended a congregation of a mainline denomination in their hometown; they now attend a large nondenominational congregation in their hometown. Suzie is a stay-at-home mom in her late thirties.

Maggie and I grew up in the same evangelical fundamentalist congregation in a very small town in the upper Midwest. She attended the same small, private liberal arts college I attended, starting as a freshman there during the fall after I graduated. She attended seminary at a large university in the Southeast, was ordained a mainline pastor, and served on the staff of a large mainline congregation in a university town also in the Southeast. In her late thirties, she is presently pastor of a congregation near her family's home in the mountain Midwest, though it is a different mainline denomination than the one in which she was ordained. Her husband is also a pastor, and they have two children.

Dana is married, in her late thirties, and the mother of two preschoolers. She lives in a medium-sized midwestern city with her pharmacist husband who came to the United States as a refugee with his family when he was a child. Dana grew up in a mainline congregation in a small town in the western Midwest, graduated from a small, private liberal arts college, and taught reading in a small, church-related boarding school for Native American children prior to graduate school. (She holds a master's degree in reading.) She currently works part-time for a public school system in a nearby town, teaching reading to children with special needs.

She and her husband attend a large, thriving congregation of a mainline denomination in the city where they live. Maggie, who was interviewed later, recommended Dana, her college roommate, for the study.

Cathy was also recommended by Maggie as an excellent candidate for this study. Maggie has known Cathy since they attended church camp and served in leadership of the denominational youth organization together many years ago. Cathy grew up in a medium-sized city in the upper Midwest and was in her late thirties at the time of the study interview. She attended a prestigious liberal arts college in the Midwest for her undergraduate degree and then earned a master's degree and PhD from a major university in the Southeast, where she met her husband. Cathy's mother was a college professor, and her father was a mainline pastor who then went on to teach and serve as dean at two seminaries and as president of a university. Cathy grew up in a mainline congregation during her childhood years and then a fundamentalist evangelical congregation during her adolescence. After a few years away from the church, she presently attends a mainline congregation in the small mountain town where she lives with her husband and preadolescent son. She is a scholar and author, writing for major mainline Christian publications.

Andie was also referred to me by Maggie. Andie is a member of the congregation where Maggie's husband is a pastor. Andie's father was in the military, and she attended a variety of very conservative congregations internationally and in the southeastern United States and mountain Midwest in towns where he was stationed. Andie attended a state university and worked as a journalist for a number of years before marrying a long-lost beau. Her husband is manager of a church camp facility where they make their home, and Andie works part-time as a freelance journalist. In her midthirties, Andie attends a downtown first church of a mainline denomination with her husband; they have a preschool-aged son.

Laurie worked at a church camp where I was on staff while in college. She then graduated from the same college I did, after majoring in business. She grew up attending an old downtown first church of a mainline denomination in a small midwestern town and now attends a more evangelical big-box church in the medium-sized city where she lives with her husband and four children. At various times over her adult life, Laurie has worked part-time outside the home. Laurie had just turned forty at the time of the study interview.

Holly is a contemporary of Laurie's, and her father taught at the college I attended. She is married with two young children and works as a nurse at the medical center where her husband is a phlebotomist in a small midwestern city. She attended seminary for a year in her twenties and is completing an advanced degree in nursing at a nearby university. She grew up attending a large old first church of a mainline denomination in a medium-sized midwestern city, and she now attends a medium-sized congregation of the same denomination with her family in the small city where they live.

Holly's husband, Kraig, is the final study participant. Kraig grew up in mainline congregations in the desert Southwest, becoming very involved in denominational youth leadership and camping as an adolescent. Kraig's early adulthood was rocky in a number of ways, but now, in his midforties, Kraig is a settled and a happy father and husband. His first career was in food service management, including a stint at the college Holly attended, which is how they met. Kraig and Holly changed careers several times over the last several years; now both are working in health care. The main reason they cite for these career changes was that job-change possibilities within their previous careers had been exhausted given that they were committed to staying in the town where they live because of their connection to the congregation of which they are a part.

PART TWO

A WAY BACK HOME

Donnie and his teenaged friends were inspired to use their gifts to start a band. They wrote and played music that motivated others to live in just and loving ways based in their Christian faith. They were really good, and their church gave them space to rehearse. The congregation was thrilled when the band was invited to play at the regional judicatory meeting in a nearby city. The members of the band were excited about the opportunity, too, and got up early to rehearse at their home church before traveling to perform at the regional meeting. They finished rehearsal early and lay down on the pews to grab a quick nap. They were awakened by the angry voice of an adult member of the congregation, chiding them for being so disrespectful as to nap in the sanctuary. Crestfallen, they packed up their gear and headed for the regional meeting to represent the congregation. Later that month they were dragged before the church elders and again reprimanded. Though some of the nine band members still write and play music, only two are still involved in church.

* * *

Mandy was excited about the invitation to teach Vacation Bible School. She had loved VBS as a child and was delighted to help others learn now that she was a teen. She met with her team teacher, the mother of one of her church friends, and together they divided up responsibilities for the week. Mandy's imagination was flooded with creative ideas and fun teaching strategies as she planned lessons for the days she would teach. She even spent some of her own money at the dollar store purchasing supplemental supplies. When the big week of VBS began, Mandy felt her first teaching experience had gone very well—until she saw the look on her team teacher's face. When Mandy finally had an opportunity to ask her teaching partner what she had done wrong, the older woman shook her head, grumbling about how she certainly wasn't going to do all that extra work and how Mandy should stick to the book. Mandy still loves to teach as a thirty-something mom, but now she focuses her creative energies on things like Girl Scouts instead of church activities.

* * *

As I analyzed interview recordings and my notes for commonalities among participant responses to questions about faith-fostering experiences during adolescence and young adulthood in their congregations, I noted that those responses could be grouped roughly into four categories. Each participant had responses that could be included in one of these four categories; many had responses that fit in each of the four. I took note as I observed these areas of redundancy beginning to emerge. For the purposes of organizing this section, I refer to these areas as:

- identity entanglements,
- still, small grown-up voices and vocations,
- the tangible grace (or sacramentality) of real relationships, and
- faithful fallowness.

Each of these areas of emphasis seemed to be a milestone along a journey that I found myself calling a way back home. The chapters in this section will each focus on one of these topics.

4

Lives Entangled with Communities of Faith

I use an intentional term—*entangled*—for this chapter. By speaking of identity entanglements, I mean to indicate something that goes beyond the role that faith typically plays in the identity formation of an adolescent. *Entanglement* is the term I choose to reflect a deep sense of comingling of identity, something that is not easily separated or sorted out.

I recognize that this term carries with it negative connotations in some contexts; however, I have chosen to reclaim the word because it is uniquely descriptive of what I found present in some very healthy ways in this study. The word describes an interconnectedness, an "all-in-ness" that is difficult to capture with other terms that could be used to describe a deep intermingling of identity. Kenda Creasy Dean lifts up research from the National Study of Youth and Religion that observes that "participating in any identity-bearing community, religious or otherwise, improves young people's likeliness to thrive."[1] What research has hinted at, I found in full, vibrant color through my conversations with some phenomenal young adults.

Let me offer some comments made by Lisa as an example of what I mean by an entanglement. On the pre-interview questionnaire (which was optional: not all study participants completed one), I asked, "What role did your youth group or church play in your teenage years? What other commitments did it rank above or below?" In answer to this question, Lisa wrote, "My identity directly connected to the church (this included youth group and church camp). It was my highest commitment, and nothing would come before it. I even set my work schedule around my church schedule so that I would not miss an event."[2]

Cathy responded to the same question in this way: "It [the church] was central for me. My closest friends, closest adult relationships. Boyfriend." When asked to rank her level of commitment to youth group or church as an adolescent, Cathy wrote: "There probably isn't a scale for that. There was no possible way I could have been more involved, emotionally or physically or spiritually."[3]

Even when the first faith community of her young adulthood was in the midst of deep conflict and theological division, Suzie's faith helped her find her way. She describes at one point how she realized, "My God is a God of grace; my God wouldn't do that," referring to the way grown-ups were acting. For Suzie, her identity was wrapped up in a God of love and grace, despite how those around her chose to act or think.[4] Suzie's experience is one of those reflected in the chapter "Calling amid Conflict" from *Greenhouses of Hope,* where Joyce Ann Mercer describes how youth are formed in faith in the midst of congregations in conflict where the faith of some withers because of the conflict and others thrive despite the circumstances.[5]

By identity entanglements, I mean to say that the young adults I spoke with described something that goes beyond including church or faith among other interests and commitments when assembling identity in adolescence and emerging adulthood. What I heard in their stories was more reflective of the way I myself have experienced key people in my life become seemingly inextricably entangled with my identity. I would not presume to offer a psychological diagnosis of this dynamic, and young adults described it to me as an intrinsic and overwhelmingly positive aspect of their faith formation.

That's why I like a reclaimed understanding of entanglement for this experiential quality. For the young adults whose stories I share here, their faith—and by extension their involvement in the church—was intrinsic to how they understood themselves. Their lives were interwoven with the lives of others whom they understood to be moving down a similar path of faith with similar goals. These young adults describe faith that was, for them, lived and intentional, not an afterthought or happenstance. Organic relationships developed with others who had similar levels of intentionality about the centrality of faith in shaping life, and those relationships played integral roles in forming identity for these young adult interviewees when they were adolescents. Because life lived in the same direction with intentionality can lead to multiple points of intersection with others who are seeking to do the same, I choose the word *entanglements* to describe the phenomenon. Unlike the similar term from psychology, *enmeshment*, which carries even more negative meanings, I intend for the word *entanglements* to describe the creative messiness of relationships these young adults identify as so crucial in allowing them to choose the alternate paths less taken in our culture. It was in the chaos and messiness of life in a congregation that these people found themselves supported and forgiven and challenged. Perhaps they couldn't appreciate the fractured character of congregational life at the time, but it seems to have been vital to their understanding of their identities within the congregation (rather than peripheral to it).

For some young adults, then, it is nearly impossible to describe who they were as adolescents or who they are today without including descriptors of active engagement with faith in the context of the local congregation. Attending closely to a couple of their stories will further inform this statement.

A Deeper Look at Identity Entanglements

Lisa's Story

Lisa thought she had discovered heaven when she first went to church camp at age twelve. A shy child, teased at school for being taller than other children her age, Lisa got to be a new person at camp. For the first time in her young life, she says, she felt acceptance. She wasn't picked on the whole week; she wasn't ostracized. In fact, she was kind of cool. At that camp, she was able to hear what her childhood years of Sunday school (in a classroom with the same kids who teased her at school) did not communicate. She heard about Jesus who wanted to be her best friend, and she says that meant everything to her. Believing that God wanted a relationship with her, that God loved and accepted her—that's what got her through some very difficult days in junior high. From then on, weekly youth group meetings carried Lisa through to the next camp or judicatory-wide youth event or youth leadership training (a denominational program).

She went to a Christian liberal arts college in a small midwestern city and expected it to be a continuation of what she had experienced at camp with the exception that she got to live there all year long—a belief she discovered later was not exactly based in reality. She majored in religion, specializing in camping ministry. During her first year, her best friend from high school, also a student at the college, was struggling with his sexual orientation. He was doing fine socially on the theologically conservative campus as long as he kept his struggle secret, but inside he was in deep pain and despair. He was losing hope that he could ever be honest about his identity and still be loved and accepted by God and others. One day he couldn't keep the secret any longer—although his coming out was sort of an accident.

Lisa's friend planned to commit suicide, and he sent notes to a number of friends through intra-campus mail so they would receive them the next day, after his suicide. Lisa suspected the planned suicide during a conversation with this friend, and when he referred to a note she would get the next day, Lisa recognized the signs and felt she needed to act. She found another student on the small campus whom she knew worked in the mailroom and had a key. When they got into the mail room and found the notes, a campus-wide search ensued to find Lisa's friend and stop the suicide. In the process, he was accidentally outed to the whole campus through a mass email sent by campus staff.

What Lisa saw happen to this lifelong friend she dearly loved was excruciating and horrifying. He was ostracized completely on the campus by a small group of people who claimed to be speaking and acting on behalf of God. Others who questioned what those few were doing just stood by, doing and saying nothing. "The person I knew wasn't what they said he was," Lisa remembers thinking. In the face of this "lynching" (Lisa's word), she felt paralyzed to do anything. She just didn't know what to do. She had been questioning her own sexual orientation in total secret for a while. She remembers with horror that she didn't stand up for her friend.[6]

Not even a year later, Lisa became clear about her sexual orientation as a woman who loved women. She was unwilling to continue to be closeted, and she remembers experiencing the same sorts of lynching behaviors she failed to speak up against when the same community took aim at her friend. I asked her what effect this had on her faith, and her response was that she "always, always felt loved by God; never abandoned." She remained a religion major at the small college, but she moved off-campus to find some safe space to be herself. She found at the college many faithful Christian professors who helped her learn how to read the Bible in ways other than literally. She learned from them that her questions were okay, that she was okay.[7] I found it remarkable to hear Lisa tell about her continued faith, in a God who created her and loved her, despite the painful ways she was treated by others.

Perhaps even more remarkable was Lisa's continued commitment to the church and to a career in camping ministry, despite the way she was treated by the campus community claiming to represent God and speak for the church. Lisa graduated and got her dream job as a full-time year-around program director of a very large camping facility in the southwestern United States. A few months into the position, after having been affirmed regularly for her good work, she was called in by her boss and fired on the spot. He made up several excuses about things "not working out" (maybe a smaller facility would be a better fit) and her not being a "team player"—lies to justify his actions. She suspected and later learned that the real reason for her termination was because he had learned she is a lesbian. She had shared in confidence in a prayer group that she and the woman she was dating were breaking up, and the information had made it back to camp management. Now the most accepting and safe place she had known (camp, referring back to her first experience of it) became the source of her greatest pain.

Lisa remembers going back to her apartment and just sitting there on her couch for a very long time—at least a whole day. In the few days prior, she had lost her romantic partner to a breakup, and now she had lost her dream job, her friends, and her safe place. Lisa shared, "I remember asking God to be there with me, just to sit with me." She remembers the only thing she could muster the energy to eat that day was a peanut-butter sandwich from the mini fridge behind the couch, which she could reach from where she was sitting. And she remembers that it felt like her first Communion experience. She felt God's presence, like God was sitting on the couch there with her, sharing in her pain.[8]

Lisa went away from church for a good long while after that, finding her way back to a local congregation with her partner years later. She asked a pastor friend whom she trusted to recommend some reconciling/affirming congregations in her city for her to visit. Lisa told me she realized at one point that she was too connected to God to leave the church, and she describes her ministry as a layperson in her congregation now as carefully chosen and selective to avoid unhealthy emotional patterns. Her faith, she says, is "very raw and real and uncomfortable and very holy." She has found ways to be a bridge for her lesbian and gay friends, helping those who are angry with God and hurt by churches to find ways to deal with their anger and hurt. "I can't be the gay person who hates the church," she says, "and I also can't be the church person who hates gays."[9]

This extended story from Lisa's life helped me to see the depth to which her identity was all tangled up with faith and the church—for better and for worse. Though her home congregation would no longer welcome her into membership as an "out" lesbian, Lisa still feels strong ties to the place that accepted her as an adolescent and formed her in faith, that recognized her gifts and affirmed her call to ministry. She says she knows they still love her, kind of like she knew God loved her and was with her that day on the couch. The congregation of her young adulthood is very different from her home church in its theology, and in that community, too, she has experienced blessing. There she has been affirmed for her gifts and invited into ministry. There she has been accepted on a deep level as she and her spouse celebrated their marriage in a sanctuary packed with church members.

Lisa's faith is deep and intrinsic to her identity—and the church as a context for living out her faith is also deeply interwoven into her identity. Given the many ways church communities hurt her, she would have easy excuses for rejecting church altogether, yet she continues to believe in it and invest herself in ministry through it. For Lisa, being an active part of a community of faith is a given: "It's just who I am." That's what I mean by an identity entanglement: a kind of life-giving interconnectedness of one's identity with a congregation that leads to a lifelong relationship.[10]

Cathy's Story

For Cathy, who grew up in a more evangelical context with an emphasis on "being good," the church with which she connected as a grown-up[11] is one she describes as comprised of people who are very real and broken, herself included. That's part of what drew her to it. Having grown up with a distinct falseness of morality, where wrongdoing took place but was carefully concealed from other church members, trying to live the impossible scripts she felt she received from the congregation of her adolescence, Cathy treasures the honesty of this congregation. She quotes her current pastor as admitting, "We don't know what we're doing here," to describe the deep mysteries of the church, such as the Eucharist. Her pastor says she's putting her money on honesty in contrast to the failed expectations of moral purity from her own youth. Cathy finds herself there too.

Between the recovering alcoholics and the recovering fundamentalists—the latter being a category Cathy uses to describe herself and the pastor—the congregation brings together a handful of people on a weekly basis to experience the poetry of the liturgy and hear their stories told in the context of the ancient stories of Scripture. Cathy found it particularly helpful early in her attendance there to hear recovering alcoholics tell their stories—something she says they have become quite reflective about through their frequent retellings at AA meetings. Hearing them rehearse their stories helped her tell her own, and in the telling, some of the toxicity she experienced in the "be good" faith of her adolescence faded. In the retelling of her story, she has also found ways to understand more clearly the authority she gave away as a youth to people who were reckless with it, preaching and teaching purity standards to youth that even they themselves did not choose to live up to.[12]

Making Sense of Identity Entanglements

As I retell the stories of Lisa and Cathy, I am aware that their stories were told to me through the lenses with which each has made meaning of those experiences. Religious expression is, after all, a meaning-making enterprise, and these two young adults not only lived these experiences but also have been wrestling with making meaning of them. And I would venture to guess that their narratives have evolved over the years as each has matured from adolescence to young adulthood.

This period that spans adolescence, emerging adulthood, and young adulthood is a time of transition between "an unexamined trust and a critically aware form of making meaning in the young adult years." Sharon Parks appropriates the work of developmentalist William G. Perry and others to describe the journey into adulthood in pursuit of differentiation, autonomy, and agency and of relation, belonging, and communion. As a person matures, Parks proposes, transitions take place in three foundational areas of their lives: (1) forms of knowing, (2) forms of dependence, and (3) forms of community. Recognizing the unique needs of those moving from adolescence into adulthood, the grown-ups in our communities of faith have a responsibility to foster growth identity (differentiation/autonomy/agency) and intimacy (relation/belonging/communion), which are key marks of this transition.

When considering identity entanglements, all three of these forms are useful, but in the case of Cathy's story, what Parks calls "forms of knowing" is a particularly helpful category. In adolescence and early adulthood, a transition takes place from what Parks calls "authority-bound" knowing through various other stages of knowing, and then finally to a place of convictional commitment. Authority-bound knowing in childhood relies almost entirely on the knowledge of others ("because I said so"). As people transition through adolescence, "because I said so" no longer works because developmentally youth are learning they have the ability to decide to which authority among the many potential authority figures in their lives they will give power. As youth accept this power to decide for themselves, there are some stages through which they move on their way to accepting full agency (say-so) for themselves—which, most learn, does not mean being one's own authority but rather wisely choosing whom to authorize.[13]

This kind of shift can be observed in Cathy's story as she moves from the authority-bound knowing of her adolescence, in the midst of assembling her identity, through periods where it felt like perhaps every authority was of equal value, now to a more considered authority-giving process that involves carefully weighing authorities through the lens of her own values. As we'll observe in chapter 7, "Faithful Fallow Times," a time away from organized religion during the period when it feels like every authority is of equal value sometimes helps. In Cathy's case, time away helped her quiet the authoritarian voices of her youth that once shouted in her mind, and enabled her to reform her faith identity with the locus of authority resting firmly in a safer place, inside herself. It seems she was clear about her identity as a child of God all along, but she needed time to modify the ways she made meaning of God's actions and to choose more selectively whom she allowed to have authority in characterizing God.

Lisa's story provides us with a similar example. Even in college and after, as she questioned her sexual orientation, Lisa herself struggled with questions of her worth as she tried to assemble an identity with forms of knowing, dependence, and community she could live with. As I hear Lisa's story, I observe that she seems to have developed strategies to adjust those forms in ways that allowed for an understanding of God and her faith that was growing and changing. She seems to have moved from forms that had become confining as her reality changed to forms that were "big enough" for her new reality and experience of God.

Lisa also had to adjust her understanding of what it meant to be part of a community, to belong. Conventional community, according to Parks, assumes conformity to a set of cultural expectations that define "us" over against "them." As conformity is challenged, a shift takes place inside young adults that typically includes a period of clinging to relationships that no longer fit very well but help us remain moored. That movement continues into a period where we realize the need for, and then create more viable networks of belonging to, communities that fit better.

For Lisa, although it took a while, this movement brought her into a community of relationships where she found mentoring and support for the person she was becoming. She remains connected to the networks of belonging from her youth, recognizing their limitations, but she invests herself in the networks of belonging that recognize who she is now and see in her the potential of who she is becoming. Parks calls these "mentoring communities," and she claims that these communities of our choosing are attractive to us because they appear to be in some way compatible with the self we feel we are becoming.[14]

For congregations, this means being intentional about getting to know the people our young adults are becoming, not confining them to their childhood and adolescent selves as we have known them previously. If we aren't paying attention, we will fall into assumptions that no longer resonate with these young adults. Because young adults may still be growing into their own sense of authority and agency, they may not yet have the strength to speak up when this happens. This is true especially with respected elders from their childhood. Frustration may grow with being confined to childhood images and, because it's easier, those young adults will simply avoid the source of the frustration and stay away from church. Additionally, congregations need to be intentional about beginning to treat young adults as the adults they are. Some simple actions like listing young adults separately from their parents in the church directory (even when they live in the same home) can send an important message of care and respect. To go beyond cosmetic changes and structure decision making to include enough space for tentative voices to share their wisdom creates important opportunities for claiming agency and voice. Such structural changes may well be helpful for not-so-young adults too. Keeping in mind that loving one another is more central to the church's mission than efficiency helps make priorities like this clearer.

While congregations can and should take important steps to foster human and faith development, particularly of younger members, what I heard in my conversations with young adults also gave me insight into

---

Paying attention means . . .
■ Asking about how someone prefers to be addressed, regardless of age (and as each one ages).
■ Speaking to younger adults as the peers they are becoming.
■ Helping people who are learning to use their voices by making it safe for them to speak up.

In practical terms, this means you might . . .
■ Recognize that little Becky now prefers to be identified as Rebecca and call her that.
■ Ask Rebecca to call you "Marion" instead of Mrs. Smith to recognize she is becoming a peer.
■ Encourage young adults and get to know them as friends.
■ Revise the church directory often to recognize the transition from youth to adulthood with a new individual entry in the directory for young adult members.

---

the personal qualities in them that contributed to resilience. In the young adults I interviewed, I saw a tenacity of faith that seemed to insinuate itself as a critical cornerstone of the new forms of knowing, dependence, and community these young adults were constructing. I heard in their stories an interconnectedness with the God of their youth that continued through their revision of these forms, and not uncritically or reflexively. I saw positive, life-giving entanglements that provided something to hold on to through the shipwrecks of emerging and young adulthood.

Notes

1. National Study of Youth and Religion, cited in Kenda Creasy Dean, *Practicing Passion: Youth and the Quest for a Passionate Church* (Grand Rapids: Eerdmans, 2004), 20.

2. Answer to question 3, page 2 of email from Lisa, received July 21, 2009.

3. Answer to questions 3 and 2, respectively, from Cathy's personal notes, September 17, 2009.

4. Author interview recording with Suzie, September 8, 2009, between minutes 20 and 25.

5. Dori Grinenko Baker, ed., *Greenhouses of Hope: Congregations Growing Young Leaders Who Will Change the World* (Herndon, VA: Alban Institute, 2010), 187.

6. Author interview recording with Lisa, September 8, 2009, between minutes 15 and 40.

7. Ibid., between minutes 21 and 28.

8. Ibid., between minutes 36 and 40.

9. Ibid., between minutes 53 and 75.

10. Ibid., between minutes 66 and 68.

11. Throughout this work, I use the term *grown-up* intentionally and specifically as an alternative to the more common term *adult*. Adulthood refers to a chronological life event; there is an age of majority in most cultures when a child becomes an adult. In using the word *grown-up*, I attempt to make a distinction between the chronological

life event that all people experience and several key marks of maturation that are critical to fostering faith in adolescents and young adults but cannot be assumed to coincide with the chronological age of majority. Some marks of a grown-up include the ability (1) to delay gratification or defer it entirely when necessary; (2) to put the needs of others first, even when it is to one's own disadvantage in some way to do so; and (3) to give of oneself with no expectation of reward in return. By this definition, some adults are not grown-ups, and some who are not yet adults might be grown-ups. Hearkening back to the Garrison Keillor quote that began chapter 1: "You don't have to be very smart to be an adult; some people prove it to you. They get promoted every year on their birthday when they ought to be held back because they still have work to do."

12. Author interview recording with Cathy, September 17, 2009, between minutes 66 and 73.

13. Sharon Daloz Parks, *Big Questions, Worthy Dreams: Mentoring Young Adults in Their Search for Meaning, Purpose, and Faith* (San Francisco: Jossey-Bass, 2000), 45, 54–69.

14. Ibid., 91–95.

5

Still, Small Voices and Vocations

Finding voice and vocation plays an important role in the lives of adolescents as they mature. Adolescents are "trying on" identities in their search for one that fits. Most youth have not yet claimed their voice or inner authority, yet this is typical developmental work that begins to take place during adolescence.[1] When they do identify their vocation, that moment of self-discovery can provide a landmark in their journey toward adulthood and a point of reference in how they learn to make meaning of their lives.

Brian Mahan, in his book *Forgetting Ourselves on Purpose: Vocation and the Ethics of Ambition*, describes vocation as a thing that often runs counter to simple ambition as a person forms a sense of what he or she is uniquely gifted to do in the world. Mahan notes that, while the most common life script focuses on financial success and power, saying, "If you get into Yale Law School, then you go to Yale Law," there are alternative scripts for life that allow for one's sense of call to override ambition. The counter scripts value connecting one's deepest passions with one's gifts and observing the response within oneself. Vocation, according to Mahan, "is less about discovering our occupation than about uncovering our preoccupations."[2] The church, in some cases but regretfully not in others, provides a context for the shaping of a vocation. The people I spoke with who had been church-active youth saw how the church, even with all of its foibles, continued to provide them with a sense of meaning and direction throughout their pursuit of vocation.

A Deeper Look at Voice and Vocation

Bill's Story

One of the stories I heard from the young adults I interviewed that most clearly illustrates this idea of the church providing meaning and direction came in a conversation with Bill. As a child, Bill was shaped by the conversations in his family about the injustices and inconsistencies of the world—conversations that explored various responses to these situations prompted by faith. As he grew into adolescence, he found himself embroiled in a constant battle with the unfairness he found in the prevailing culture. Bill talked about getting a little lost in his anger at this unfairness, particularly when he was consistently disempowered by broken adults in his life, such as school and civic officials who behaved like bullies. This drove Bill into countercultural communities where he felt safer and accepted, such as a group of skateboard enthusiasts his age. These communities brought with them some unhelpful patterns of behavior, as well, and Bill was introduced to alcohol and marijuana as a means to escape and soothe his anger and pain. He struggled with bouts of depression when the lostness and pain became too great.

In my conversation with Bill, he talked about how taking action on justice issues because of his faith had been an important part of his preadolescent years. At the time, he saw it as part of who he was. After the bumpiness of his adolescent years, Bill describes the time when things inside him started to get sorted out in this way: "I came home to myself then." So central to his identity was the idea that people of faith work for justice that he reconnected with something essential about himself through intentional work for justice while he was still in the morass of floundering to form an identity. Off and on in his final years of college, Bill was able to find people who shared his sense of mission, which gave him enough hope to get clean and establish a sense of stability.

As a result of this vocational awareness, Bill felt motivated in his midtwenties to connect with other people of faith seeking justice. He wasn't really looking for a church, but he knew that was a place to start looking for others who cared about justice. He found his way to the first congregation of his young adulthood: a downtown church in the large northwestern US city where he lived, a place where he became involved in justice ministries and volunteered with at-risk youth (like he had been). With a detour through a year of seminary to develop the tools he need-ed to think theologically and articulate his passions, eventually this pre-occupation with justice helped Bill find his vocation as an attorney in advocacy and justice work.[3]

Something to live for. Our language seems to indicate that we think of time much like money—as something we have a limited amount of and must choose how to "spend." Adolescents and young adults, with lives to "spend" at their discretion, look to invest their lives in things that mat-ter—that's what I heard from the young adults I interviewed, and from countless other adolescents and young people I've worked with over the years. The "to die for" imagery developed by Kenda Creasy Dean in her book *Practicing Passion* (described more fully in chapter 2), is clever and catchy, but it doesn't adequately capture the yearnings of those whose stories I heard. In their lives, I heard passionate people querying their world, hungry for something to invest in that's worth their lifetime of work—that is, something *to live for*. A deeper look at a couple of inter-view stories offers a context for further exploration of these ideas.

Dana's Story

Another young adult who testified to the ways in which she found her still-forming and increasingly mature voices and vocations is Dana, who grew up in a small mainline congregation in the western Midwest where she participated in the church's very small youth group. She says her fam-ily was faithful and active in participation throughout her life, to the extent that participating in worship and youth group weren't optional in her family.

Dana began attending a denominational camp in fifth grade. Both the camping experience and the friends she made there became very impor-tant to her. They offered her glimpses into other ways of living her faith, alternatives to the ways of living one's faith that she found in her home church. Though she was an active participant in her church through her childhood, Dana's faith and the church she grew up in became "hers" in new ways during adolescence. During this period, she began to assemble for herself a life of faith based on the alternative scripts she found through camp and region youth events. Dana reflects that, even prior to becoming an adult, she had always been "more than just a youth," by which she meant she took seriously her church membership to the point of leading in her youth group, serving on church committees, attending business meetings, voting on issues, and so on in ways that most people her age did not. That being said, Dana still felt that she couldn't speak up, especially at congregational meetings; she wasn't confident of the value of what she would say, so she mostly kept quiet but present.[4]

Dana describes a situation during her first semester in college when she was visiting back home and found her voice in the congregation. She describes a congregational meeting called hastily while the pastor of her Baptist congregation was away on vacation. Essentially, she says, it was a meeting where dissatisfied members would be able to get an audience to trash the pastor's work and character, fomenting an ouster of the pastor with whom they disagreed because of his heavy community leadership and service involvement. In the meeting, Dana recalls being appalled at how badly these grown-ups were behaving, not at all like the Christian elders she believed they were growing up. Dana finally understood that simply being chronologically adult didn't necessarily mean maturity in faith. She mustered the courage and confidence and spoke up at the meeting, calling out the "grown-ups" for their behavior and the unfair tactics they were using.

For Dana, this incident was pivotal in claiming her voice, and it accelerated her vocational quest, as well. The act of speaking up was critical to her growth, almost irrespective of the response she received from those at the meeting. In the years that followed, she found herself drawn to service and justice work, particularly serving as a teacher (for little compensation) at a rural Native American boarding school and later volunteering countless hours with cleanup efforts when the city in which she lived as a graduate student experienced serious floods.

Subsequently, her vocation took her to serve in inner-city Chicago, in Africa, and in Honduras on mission trips. Having earned a master's degree in reading, Dana had strong encouragement from her mentors to continue for a PhD, but she chose to set aside that option, at least for a while, in favor of hands-on work with children. She taught exceptional and gifted children in the small city where she lives for a few years, but now finds more meaning teaching children with reading difficulties in a rural midwestern school district.

Dana's sense of vocational identity included a sense of what it meant to be a person of faith. Being a person a faith brought with it investment in the church's life as modeled by her parents, and this led to Dana claiming her voice on behalf of those unable to advocate for themselves. Finding her sense of agency in this way helped her to see her vocation connected to working for justice for all. Her life doesn't follow the script prevalent in popular culture—and she traces the course of her life today back to the time when she spoke up for what she believed was right to a bunch of grown-ups she'd known all her young life who were not living up to the faith they claimed.[5]

Tonya's Story

Tonya grew up in a home with alcoholics. She describes figuring out that home was not a safe place at a very early age, and then how she developed coping strategies to help her and her sisters survive. Church, which she attended with her grandmother, became a safe place for her to escape the craziness in the rest of her life. Having to look out for herself and her younger siblings as a child, Tonya developed some grown-up insights and skills for survival while she was still a kid.

Tonya describes volunteering at the local Goodwill during two teenage summers—on top of all her other responsibilities and her regular job. When people encountered her there, adults and youth alike were surprised and asked what she did to get into legal trouble that got her sentenced to do community service hours, because they couldn't imagine that she would just willingly volunteer. While volunteering did provide an excuse to be somewhere other than home, Tonya describes service as "just part of who I am."

Tonya also told me about being one of two kids her age (the other was the pastor's son) at church during her eighth grade year, which meant attending a two-student Sunday school class. Rather than attend that awkwardly small class or skip Sunday school altogether, Tonya created a Sunday school class for some preteen "naughty kids" who had been kicked out of regular Sunday school (at this and several other congregations in town). Tonya came up with the idea, and the church supported her by providing the space and approval, and by purchasing curriculum of her choosing from the local Christian bookstore for her to use.

Tonya describes a passion she had for troubled kids and her "knack" for working with them because she learned in her own alcoholic home to value truth and authenticity—important qualities for dealing with kids with behavior issues. She developed her skills as a young babysitter for her troubled cousins and other children in her own family. Years later Tonya continues to use the gifts she first discovered in her home church. Today she serves as a foster-parent-turned-adoptive-parent and as a coordinator of a program her church created that helps preteen girls from homes like hers develop self-esteem and career skills. Tonya's home congregation fanned the spark of her still, small voice and vocation, which now burns strong as she advocates for and mentors girls.[6]

Making Sense of Still, Small Voices and Vocations

In *Greenhouses of Hope*, in her chapter entitled "Staying Awake," Margaret Ann Crain describes the way in which people in the congregation she studied help one another in their individual journeys. Simply by consciously using language of vocation and call continuously and in key moments throughout their lives, the church helps their youth come to understand themselves in light of their Christian vocation. Crain describes a "year-round cycle of community forma-tion, mission immersion, theological reflection on life experience, and liturgical affirmation of the community's role" in the lives of members across generations.[7]

In my conversations with Dana, Tonya, Bill, and others, I observed that few of the congregations they described came close to living up to the intentionality with which Crain's congregation undertook vocation-al formation. However, it seems that even bumbling attempts and a will-ingness to make space for youth to explore and experiment seem to have had an effect in the lives of the people in my study. For example, in the church Crain studied, in addition to providing typical opportunities for youth outside the congregation, such as mission trips and camping min-istry, the usual age/status hierarchies within the congregation were aban-doned in favor of offering youth opportunities to lead alongside the adult members. In contrast, while the young adults I interviewed seemed to indicate a less-than-ideal level of openness among their church's adults to their adolescent leadership, even that minimal openness made a difference as they wrestled with vocation.

Paying attention means . . .

■ Valuing the unique gifts and perspectives of people at many stages of life.

■ Inviting people into servant leadership in the congregation based on gifts and vocation, rather than longevity or seniority.

In practical terms, this means you might . . .

■ Invite gifted leaders to serve on the church council with a balance of different ages.

■ Incorporate children, youth, and adults of all ages in worship lead-ership according to their gifts.

■ Create covenants of behavior and smaller discussion groups during business meetings so all can be heard.

To better understand what is taking place in the emerging adults' search for vocation, we'll need a closer look at both how we understand vocation and how young adults describe their meaning-making journey. James Fowler, famous for his work describing stages of faith development, puts right the mistaken conflation of vocation and work. He writes, "Vocation, seen as a call to partnership with God on behalf of the neighbor, constitutes a far more fruitful way to look at the question of our specialness, our giftedness, and our possibilities of excellence."[8] Taken in this way, vocation becomes not just something we figure out individually but something we uncover in community as God works in and through us. For people of faith, vocation becomes a significant way in which they make meaning of their lives. If this idea of vocation seems foreign, perhaps it's because the pervasive myth in the dominant culture in the United States is that work is an individual thing and successes are earned.[9]

In many ways, the stories I have offered in this chapter reflect less-than-ideal situations in which these young people quested for voice and vocation. Most were tolerated in their churches more than they were encouraged. Most had more models of how not to live the Christian life than how to live it. Most had inadequate and faltering support from their communities of faith. Yet, despite the brokenness of their congregations, the young adults I spoke with clearly found enough of what they needed when they needed it. Their stories correlate with existing research by testifying that youth can and do discern vocation in life-altering ways, even in challenging circumstances.

Notes

1. Mary Field Belenky, Blythe McVicker Clinchy, Nancy Rule Goldberger, Jill Mattuck Tarule, *Women's Ways of Knowing: The Development of Self, Voice, and Mind* (New York: Basic Books, 1986), 54.

2. Brian J. Mahan, *Forgetting Ourselves on Purpose: Vocation and the Ethics of Ambition* (San Francisco: Jossey-Bass, 2002), 183.

3. Author interview recording with Bill, March 27, 2009, between minutes 28 and 29.

4. Author interview recording with Dana, December 29, 2009, between minutes 70 and 73.

5. Ibid., between minutes 30 and 47.

6. Author interview recording with Tonya, March 26, 2009, between minutes 10 and 21.

7. Margaret Ann Crain, "Staying Awake," in Dori Grinenko Baker, ed., *Greenhouses of Hope: Congregations Growing Young Leaders Who Will Change the World* (Herndon, VA: Alban Institute, 2010), 48–49.

8. James Fowler, *Becoming Adult, Becoming Christian: Adult Development and Christian Faith* (San Francisco: Harper & Row, 1984), 102.

9. Dori Grinenko Baker and Joyce Ann Mercer, *Lives to Offer: Accompanying Youth on Their Vocational Quests* (Cleveland, OH: Pilgrim, 2007), 163.

6

Tangible Grace
in Real Relationships

The word I really want to use in describing this experiential quality of tangible grace is *sacramentality.* Coming out of a Baptist tradition, I know the term is loaded with doctrinal differences, so let me unpack what I mean in using the term. At its most basic level, *sacrament* refers to a means of grace, a human practice that makes tangible God's grace. I use the term to reflect the depth of the power of genuine relationships in the lives of adolescents, both with others their age and with grown-ups in the congregation. For the young adults who graced me with their stories, real relationships were of critical importance throughout their lives.

By "real relationships," I mean to indicate that it wasn't the superficial relationships—the "niceness" of church—that made a difference in the lives of these young adults. Rather, they deeply valued the honest and messy friendships that grow among people who take risks together and invest in one another and sometimes need to ask forgiveness for mistakes (and then apologize when it's called for). In those kinds of relationships, I see the human embodiment of God's grace, where people and relationships become a means of grace. This is the heart of the tangible grace—the sacramentality—of real relationships. In the experiences described for me by young adults, I learned about the importance of things like serving others together and table fellowship and passing the peace each week—how these practices that re-member each participant, centering them in who God created them to be as beloved children of God.

Faith is about relationship. Narratives of relationship can be found throughout Scripture. In the biblical stories of Jacob and Esau, David and Jonathan, Elijah and Elisha, Ruth and Naomi, we hear of relationships that mattered deeply in the lives of these people. God's interactions with humanity prioritize relationships; consider the covenants God made with Abraham and David as examples. We hear about the centrality of relationship in Jesus' teachings, as well. Consider that Jesus said "where two or three are gathered in my name, I am there among them" (Matthew 18:20). Jesus supplemented the first commandment, "To love the Lord your God," with a second, which he said was like the first, namely, to "love your neighbor as yourself" (Matthew 22:37, 39; Mark 12:30, 31). We hear the centrality of relationship reflected again in the Pauline epistles in the description of the church as an interconnected body with many parts working together (1 Corinthians 12). In relationships, God's gift of grace can be shared in tangible ways. This section looks at a number of ways that relationships function in an interconnected fashion with faith, identity formation, and the willingness of emerging adults to retain or reclaim connection with the church.

As an adolescent, Cathy remembers that the families of other youth her age at church were important: "Those families enclosed us." She went on to describe those adults as being "like second parents to me." Given that her own parents were important role models for her, Cathy's description of these other, unrelated adults is significant. She talked about how, as teens, they were given space to be loud and silly and, at times, arrogant about their own understanding and abilities. Looking back on the time, she says she felt loved, as if the community understood itself as having a purpose in the lives of their youth members.

As a teenager, Cathy says she probably thought that doctrinal consensus was what united her congregation. But when she experienced the theology of the church of her adolescence becoming too confining, Cathy began to realize that the support she cherished from the church of her adolescence didn't reside in conforming to a set of rigid theological understandings as she once believed—the support was in the community's intentional relationships of love and care for her and her peers. As Cathy separated these two—unity of belief and supportive relationships—in her own mind, she grew to understand that it was the supportive relationships that she valued most, and those relationships could be found in a congregation with greater theological and other diversity.[1]

My conversations with other young adults resonated with Cathy's story. Suzie told me that as a teenager she noticed that the adults without kids helped out with youth group events when they didn't have to. She says that over time this made those adults feel like extended family.[2] Her brother Morris concurred, describing the way the larger congregation "claimed us, nurtured us, involved us."[3] Lisa also remembers the extra adults who helped with youth group—people who supported, valued, and "really mostly tolerated us."[4]

In my interviews, I was struck by the number of times, having asked about church people who had been important to them when they were teenagers, I heard stories of unnamed faithful grown-ups who simply offered consistent presence in their lives as they grew in faith. In their book *Lives to Offer: Accompanying Youth on Their Vocational Quests*, Dori Grinenko Baker and Joyce Ann Mercer describe this as companioning and identify it as a posture critical for ministry, especially in adolescence. They tell the story of a group of adults and confirmation-aged youth who together experienced walking a labyrinth for the first time. Although the adults were uncertain of the experience much as the youth were, their presence upheld the youth as the adults walked just ahead of them, figuring out this new terrain as they went. The adults had the added benefit of being able to use their broader experience and well-used grown-up tool kit to do so. They provided hope and inspiration for the youth as they, too, found their way through this new experience of a new path.[5]

As I discovered in my interviews, companioning has to do with more than just "being there" and sharing the stuff of life, but rather involves intentionally journeying together, being on the move, going somewhere on purpose and going together. Even more interesting to me was that the young adults' stories of faithful companions and "presencers" continued as study participants described the churches of their young adult-hood. This connection felt too important to ignore.

What Baker and Mercer call companioning reminded me of a similar phenomenon called the zone of proximal development (ZPD). The idea was first posed by L. S. Vygotsky, writing in Russia in the early twentieth century. The ZPD is the area between what someone can do alone and what that individual can do with assistance from someone who has already gained competency in that task or skill. Adolescents need to be around people who have themselves worked through at least some of the issues facing teenagers and who can help youth envision and take next develop-mental steps. The role of these adults is to stand alongside adolescents and, with intentionality, assist by example through direct and conscious interaction as adolescents take their next developmental and faith steps.[6] Examples of the ZPD at work can be found in the experiences described by many of the young adults who shared their stories with me.

Andie pointed to a woman she met when on a mission trip in a flood-ed area of the upper Midwest. Andie described how they were cleaning up what was left of this elderly woman's home, all of it encased in smelly, nasty river muck. The home and everything in it was a total loss. As the volunteer group of which Andie was a part began to clean up the mess, they asked the woman, who was too frail to go into her flooded home herself, if there was anything she especially wanted them to retrieve. Andie was thinking of valuables, important papers, and the like, but the woman told them that the only thing she really wanted was a plastic nativity set her husband gave her for their first Christmas together. Her husband had died the year prior.

At first Andie was flummoxed by the woman's statement. There was certainly more valuable stuff in the woman's house than this plastic nativi-ty. Didn't she want them to salvage her TV if they could, or perhaps dish-es or silver or family photos? Then something clicked for her and Andie realized "She's got it all figured out." That was the incident that started Andie thinking about alternative scripts for her life, about other ways of thinking about success, about vocation and what it meant for her to serve

God. This elderly woman provided the model for Andie of a life in which meaning came primarily from relationships and less from possessions.[7]

Cathy told of an experience in which I see ZPD at work , in her case with a youth pastor. Though she would not have spoken of her experience of her adolescent congregation in this way growing up, Cathy now reflects on her experience there as one that set up unreal expectations for morality, something she describes with the euphemism "being good and beautiful." In her college years, Cathy's reaction to this shallow definition of faithfulness was that she "went looking for a version of 'the rules' that you could actually follow." But even in high school, Cathy was drawn to her youth pastor, whom she experienced as "very real" in the midst of the "unreal" environment of surface morality of which she was increasingly aware in the congregation. This youth pastor opened a door just far enough to allow Cathy to see the possibility of another way of understanding herself as a person of faith. This youth pastor showed Cathy something she held on to during the deep purging of surface morality she undertook over her emerging adult years. Cathy sees now that the youth pastor of her adolescence, still a friend, holds largely the same set of beliefs that Cathy has since replaced with ones she finds more life-giving. That said, her youth pastor provided the "scaffolding" (a euphemism given to Vygotsky's ZPD by later theorists) to allow Cathy to take what were crucial next steps at the time.[8]

A Deeper Look at the Sacramentality of Real Relationships

Maggie's Story

Maggie describes feeling like there were few people in her home church that she would have described as models for her of how to grow in faith if that didn't mean believing certain things and living by a strict moral code—which didn't feel much like a real relationship with a loving God to her. Her response to the role models held up by her congregation growing up was that they seemed to Maggie like a bunch of pretty needy adults. "I could do 'grown-up' better than that," she recalls think-ing as a teenager.

For Maggie, grown-ups she met at church camp, and even more so, professors at the church-related college she attended, provided satisfy-ing models for her of deep faith that was filled with questions. Maggie recalls being grateful to learn from them some options for ways to express faith that fit her better. She describes this process in college as becoming "more spiritual" as she spent time writing and reflecting on the deep mysteries of faith with professors who became trusted friends. In contrast to her home church, Maggie describes the feeling-experience of the church of her young adulthood as "the regular and marked response to God's grace." As she grew into young adulthood, faith became more integrated into her life and less something she did every week (and twice on Sundays) at church.

The church of her adolescence disregarded Maggie's growing sense of call to ministry, but she knew they loved and cared for her in the lim-ited ways they knew how. As she moved through seminary and into min-istry, she emulated the paths she learned from those who honored her discernment process and celebrated her giftedness. A mentoring com-munity, which was diffuse in the case of the camp friends and more intentional in the case of the college professors, played an essential role in Maggie's development and growth in faith.[9]

Sharon Daloz Parks, in her book *Big Questions, Worthy Dreams*, describes the way mentoring communities intentionally foster faith for-mation in young people. She describes qualities such as a network of belonging; big-enough questions; habits of the mind; worthy dreams; and access to key images, concepts, and practices. Through these inter-views I saw how, although not every adolescent or emerging adult has the benefit of mentors and mentoring communities that embody all of these qualities, these communities of which they are a part do fulfill some of aspects of these roles, even if they do it only some of the time.[10] Maggie wasn't the only interviewee who identified grown-ups who showed the way as those young adults encountered wider communities and discovered bigger questions that helped them take next steps developmentally. For many, it seems mentors *do* matter; however, such mentors represent only a small fraction of the people in a congregation. Young adults told me about other people across generations whom they would not have considered mentors but who still had a positive impact on the growth of their faith in adolescence and beyond.

One example, shared by Laurie, was of a camp counselor who challenged her faith profoundly. Essentially this person helped her ask the larger, more honest questions that were under the surface, not yet given voice—questions she hadn't heard raised in her faith community back home.[11] Similarly, Andie shared an experience that she had with two mature journalist colleagues she met during her summer internship in college. "They were not believers," she said by way of characterizing their faith, but then she went on to describe how they were people she knew valued truth and ethics, and they helped her see through people's intentions.[12]

Holly and Kraig's Story

For Holly and Kraig, the idea of mentoring communities resonated deeply with their experiences in young adulthood. Holly and Kraig both described experiencing mentoring communities in the churches of their young adulthood and came to value that role very much. For both of them, a parent was entering ministry during their adolescence, so they experienced being well-known in the congregation of their youth, having lots of connections with people, despite not knowing any of them all that well.

As adults in their current church, Holly and Kraig each, separately, shared how they had an immediate (albeit somewhat artificial) connection to the members because many of them were alumni of the college where Holly and Kraig had met. That made joining the church feel "like coming home" because of the many contacts and friends they knew in common. As those relationships grew and became more genuine, they found in this new congregation a mentoring community they valued deeply, to such an extent that they have changed careers in order to stay in this small city where they found a faith home. The network of belonging in the mentoring community of their congregation has become vitally important in their lives. They hope it will be for their children as they mature, as well.[13]

Making Sense of Tangible Grace in Real Relationships

A who's who of scholars has identified the importance of real relationship through things like mentoring communities (Parks) and companioning (Baker/Mercer) and scaffolding (Vygotsky). Mark DeVries posited nearly two decades ago that adolescents need the church to function as a kind of extended family—something Kenda Creasy Dean and Ron Foster lifted up a few years later in their research.[14] My conversations with young adults seemed to amplify this idea, suggesting that even something as simple as "being there" matters. The better the quality of the "being there," I would argue, the more impact the supportive presence has on the likelihood that youth will grow up having integrated faith as a critical part of their identity and having their voice and vocation fostered by nurturing structures within the local congregation.

Maria Harris, in her book *Fashion Me a People*, describes how the central elements or key practices of the church embody the entire course of its life. She argues that since the church is a people with a mission and ministry, then it must take seriously the ways in which each of the forms its mission and ministry takes is educative. Essentially, Harris proposes, everything in the course of the church's life teaches, from preaching to hospitality, from mission/service to prayer—a statement that has far-reaching implications. If everything teaches, it follows that everyone is both teacher and learner.[15]

Seen through this lens, those people on the sidelines in the congregation who may not think they are teaching anything or involved in ministry with youth are simply wrong. How these "nonteaching" adults live out their faith matters more than they could imagine. Youth and emerging adults are constantly observing the lives of adults, looking for models (and inconsistencies). Congregations will commonly support sending their youth on mission trips and service projects that

Paying attention means . . .

■ Modeling mutual respect across generations, while allowing each person to discern the trusted individuals who have *earned* respect.

■ Expecting older adults to care about the church thriving beyond their own lifetimes.

■ Learning about the particular needs of people across the life cycle and caring for those needs.

■ Creating safe space to discuss difficult issues and working together to enforce the safety of that space for all.

■ Trusting the God of our foremothers and forefathers to continue gifting the next generations, too.

■ Making places of discernment and questioning within life-giving traditions.

■ Honoring the good intentions of one another, even as we risk sharing honestly about how those efforts are received.

In practical terms, this means you might . . .

■ Encourage young adults and get to know them as friends.

■ Create covenants of behavior and smaller discussion groups during business meetings so all can be heard.

■ Offer learning opportunities for people of all ages based on their interests and passions in addition to, or instead of, their age-range or marital and family status.

■ Invite people across the life cycle to serve in roles in the congregation based on their gifts rather than their ages.

■ Foster friendships across generations by offering opportunities for interaction with people of a variety of ages (small groups, etc.).

■ Offer educational programs to help people of various ages understand the unique challenges, needs, and joys of each period of the life cycle.

most adults in the congregation don't participate in. But formation through service is not just good for youth; service projects also provide vital opportunities for growth and relationship-building for all ages. Teaching and learning in formal settings is essential at all ages for the health of the community of faith. Worship or preaching or even Communion—things sometimes reserved for grown-ups—form children's faith in key ways.

The stories I heard from young adults about the importance of the seeming bystanders in their congregations informs our understanding of the level to which community matters. We have known that mentoring matters. We have come to understand the way in which scaffolding can help people take their next developmental (and faith) steps. We have become aware of the importance of intentionally walking alongside one another in the faith practice called companioning. We have become aware of the depth of impact relationships have, which become a means of tangible grace in the lives of youth and young adults.

Through the testimony of these young adults, we are also hearing that no one in the congregation should assume that seeming bystanders don't matter when it comes to impacting the lives of the youth of the congregation. Just being there matters! And the quality of the "being there" affects the impact. Intentional faith formation is important for everyone—not just for their own spiritual well-being, but for the spiritual health of future generations. Faith formation is of vital importance. Perhaps we could have a new motto for faith formation in our congregations: "If you won't do it for your own spiritual health, then do it for the kids!" Practicing what we preach and preaching what we practice matters more than we know!

Notes

1. Author interview recording with Cathy, September 17, 2009, between minutes 26 and 30.

2. Author interview recording with Suzie, September 8, 2009, between minutes 12 and 15.

3. Author interview recording with Morris and Tonya, March 26, 2009, between minutes 25 and 37.

4. Author interview recording with Lisa, September 8, 2009, between minutes 15 and 17.

5. Dori Grinenko Baker and Joyce Ann Mercer, *Lives to Offer: Accompanying Youth on Their Vocational Quests* (Cleveland, OH: Pilgrim, 2007), 19–20.

6. L. S. Vygotsky, *Mind in Society: The Development of Higher Psychological Processes* (Cambridge, MA: Harvard University Press, 1978), 84–85.

7. Author interview recording with Andie, September 2, 2009, between minutes 16 and 32.

8. Author interview recording with Cathy, September 17, 2009, around minute 31 and between minutes 55 and 85.

9. Author interview recording with Maggie, September 2, 2009, between minutes 6 and 30.

10. Sharon Daloz Parks, *Big Questions, Worthy Dreams: Mentoring Young Adults in Their Search for Meaning, Purpose, and Faith* (San Francisco: Jossey-Bass, 2000), 135.

11. Author interview recording with Laurie, September 4, 2009, between minutes 14 and 16.

12. Author interview recording with Andie, September 2, 2009, between minutes 16 and 32.

13. Author interview recording with Holly and Kraig, September 5, 2009, between minutes 80 and 93.

14. Mark DeVries, *Family-Based Youth Ministry: Reaching the Been-There, Done-That Generation* (Downers Grove, IL: InterVarsity, 1994). See also Kenda Creasy Dean and Ron Foster, *The Godbearing Life: The Art of Soul Tending for Youth Ministry* (Nashville: Upper Room, 1998), 77–85.

15. Maria Harris, *Fashion Me a People: Curriculum in the Church* (Louisville: Westminster John Knox, 1989), 16–17, 43.

7

Faithful Fallow Times

While a handful of the young adults I interviewed found their way to churches all along the journey from adolescence into young adulthood, most described a period of time when they were not active in a congregation. Some chose this time away while others became de-churched when the congregations they had chosen changed in ways untenable to them, and vice versa. While some of us might think this time away from church would have represented a period of decreased spirituality and faithfulness, I heard in their stories a deep and genuine faith in a God with whom they were in relationship all along. This may have been a fallow period for them in terms of active participation in a congregation, but in several cases it represented a period of growth that produced a more honest and richly textured spirituality. There was, indeed, faithfulness in the fallow time.

Tethered in the Fallow Time

Cathy describes the lovely freedom she felt during a time in her life when she didn't attend church. Starting Sundays slowly, drinking coffee, and reading the *New York Times* in bed were things she learned to enjoy, and things that provided for a time of re-creation and Sabbath in her overbusy week. Still, she says, she missed the poetry of the liturgy, the sense of transcendence in prayer and Eucharist, and connecting with "something bigger than me."

At several points during this fallow time, Cathy found herself drawn to the local agency that provided meals for those in need wherever she was living at the time. One of the steps of living into her grown-up faith was recognizing her passion to provide food for hungry people. She told me that "it became more important than any church" had been in her life. In her soup kitchen work, there was none of the ego or pride or morality that had become toxic for Cathy growing up in the church; she cooked and people had something to eat. Letting go of "the rules" as her primary means of relating to God meant letting go of almost everything related to church for Cathy, except this one thing—serving at the local soup kitchen. And it was that one thing that kept her tethered to her faith during her fallow years and helped her find her way back into a congregation as an adult.[1]

Holly and Kraig each describe periods away from involvement with a congregation, but after their marriage they admitted to each other that they both missed church. Neither had felt comfortable visiting churches as single adults; it was always awkward. "It [visiting a church] was something we could do together," Holly explained, which made her feel safer and made the process easier.[2]

Kraig notes that during his adolescence, he became deeply involved in the youth group of a local congregation and beyond, even serving on local, district, and conference-level boards and committees. Late in Kraig's adolescence, his father (who had become a lay pastor during Kraig's childhood) was fired from his church job, "over something stupid," as Kraig remembers it. Because of that incident, Kraig lost all interest in church: "Suddenly church looked like politics to me, not faith."

In the next few years, in the midst of the "crazy family stuff" and self-abusive behaviors of his emerging adulthood in the desert Southwest, Kraig remembered something important about himself on a visit (which became a relocation) to a frozen northern plains state in the middle of winter. On one of his first nights there, Kraig went to a bar for a drink and accidentally forgot all his money on a table when he walked away to play pool with some local guys. When he came back, the money was all still right where he'd left it. "People were kind to each other, really genuinely nice," Kraig recalls as he notes that folks he didn't know waved to him from passing cars and invited him along on hunting trips. "It felt like church," he reflected. This was an important intersection in Kraig's journey of faith as he encountered something he had known as an adolescent and that made him long for "the support of a church family to live in healthy ways."[3]

Kraig and Holly both changed careers rather than relocate from the town where they had lived for fifteen years—a town they moved to partly because the church they had visited during an interview weekend for new jobs in the area was so welcoming. They speculated that perhaps the fear of not having the support of a healthy church family is what has kept them there. "Why would I risk that purposefully?" Kraig asks rhetorically. Both acknowledge the pain they experienced because of churches at certain times in their lives, which dissipated with some time away. They were ready for connections again when they relocated to this town, and the congregation there "felt like going home" for both of them.

Holly reflects that in her family growing up, church involvement was a given for her: "It's what you do—you go to church." Faith and involvement with a community of faith is deeply a part of who she is once again as a young adult—so much so that she and Kraig can't imagine their lives without it. "We got lucky," Holly observes, "we got our invitation."[4]

Faithful without a Fallow Time

For Andie, Laurie, and Dana, there was no real break in their active involvement with congregations, although each noted separately that they chose to become involved in very different congregations as young adults from those of their childhoods. In each case, this was initially because of school- or work-related relocations, but Andie is an example of someone who lives once again as a young adult in the city where she graduated from high school. Andie and her fiancé (now her husband) attended his church together in the months prior to their wedding because of a young adult small group Bible study led by a retired pastor and his wife. While it was tempting to go back to the church of her adolescence, "where everybody knew her name" (to paraphrase the old theme song from *Cheers*), Andie felt really connected to the young adult group because the leaders fostered an atmosphere where everyone felt known and loved. Her family taught her by example that "there are no benchwarmers" in a church family, and she is investing herself in this congregation even as she wrestles with questions of identity and vocation as a new stay-at-home mother.[5]

For Laurie, getting married right out of college to a person also committed to faith, and having their wedding at the church they attended together in college, meant getting involved in that church for a while after college and marriage. The small-group Bible study for young adults, led by the same pastor and spouse who retired to Andie's area, helped Laurie and her husband connect in the congregation as grown-ups. When that pastor retired (not entirely by his choice), Laurie's family, which now included children, felt disenfranchised by the politics that had forced the pastoral change. But they never really considered just not participating in a church.

They visited the congregation where Laurie worked as bookkeeper, and both felt like this new congregation needed gifts and abilities they had. For Laurie, who felt as a child as if the church was "her" church, this congregation has been a place with enough theological space and missional options for all the members of their family to find a place to learn and serve. Laurie sums up her involvement in a congregation as a desire they have for their children, "to see faith lived in [the children's] lives," not just a desire for them to have a religious upbringing.[6]

Dana describes finding a place in some congregation everywhere she moved as a young adult, from small rural towns with women's Bible study and Jell-O at potlucks, to the congregation where she connected initially so she would have a place to get married in the city where she now lives. While some of the various congregations did a better job than others of welcoming her as a single adult in their midst, she still found ways to connect in almost every one of them. She recognizes that she actively looked for those connections. But whether she was feeling connected or not, Dana attended nearly every Sunday. And she compensated for the churches that didn't meet all her needs by pursuing supplemental ministry experiences; she went on international mission trips and did local community service with friends' churches, for example.

The congregation of her young adulthood—the one she joined so she could get married and raise her family there—is a place that reached out to her, got to know her, and invited her to get involved. As a mother of young children for whom direct community service is tricky to fit into her schedule right now, Dana found a place in the congregation on the social outreach committee that plans a couple of fundraisers a year and gives away the proceeds to local agencies in which the congregation is involved in some hands-on way (including a school in Africa). Dana reflects that in most cases other adults invited her into the churches of her young adulthood, but she also went into the relationships expecting to do her part in each church family, expecting to find her place. Going into a new church intentionally looking for a place to serve, she thinks, helped her find a place in each church.[7]

A Deeper Look at Faithful Fallowness

Morris and Tonya's Story

When Morris and Tonya found themselves de-churched, Tonya wondered, "What's wrong with us that we don't fit in?" Both had a brief period where they were away from regular congregational involvement, but then, during their engagement and early marriage, they attended the church where Morris had grown up. Morris played guitar with the worship team, and together they became involved with youth and children's ministries, which had been so important to them growing up. Then a pastoral change allowed a more conservative faction of the congregation to grow in power and make changes that were untenable to them.

Morris remembered inclusive language in worship while he was growing up, so he took note when exclusively male language for God and humanity became the standard in worship. Tonya felt pressure to teach from a particular theological perspective in children's and youth programming as the curriculum resources were shifted to those produced by more conservative publishing houses. Morris's parents stopped attending the church in which they had been deeply invested their whole adult lives. Eventually Morris and Tonya felt they had to leave too. They church shopped off and on for about six months before they finally became discouraged and just dropped the issue for a while. When asked what they were looking for, Tonya recalls their list included "welcoming, inviting, not cliquey, not mega, not old/dead/tired, not too big, not too charismatic." They realized this was a tall order and largely in the "eye of the beholder."

Some other former members of that congregation who were also de-churched, including Morris's parents, started meeting as a small group over a potluck dinner on Sunday evenings in one another's homes. The group was led by a woman from their old congregation who was attending seminary; Tonya didn't like how "radical" she seemed. While Tonya and Morris were both pretty sure that this kind of loosely connected group would not be the right fit for them, they went a couple of times, mostly to please Morris's parents. They were completely surprised by how much they both enjoyed the gathering. Tonya came to find images she could relate to in what once felt radical to her. Eventually they were part of chartering a new congregation that grew out of these gatherings.

It was energizing for both Tonya and Morris to be part of the new congregation and to be challenged to think theologically about what it meant to be church, to consider what was essential. The new congregation included, as part of its by-laws, a provision that it cannot own property, for example. Rather than invest in property, the group decided to invest intentionally in people. This was a guideline that arose as they wrestled together with how buildings can become an excuse that keeps people from doing hands-on ministry with their neighbors and in their communities. The new congregation was intentionally inclusive, providing safe space for those who were hurt by other congregations and nurturing questions and ongoing reflections about faith along the journey of life.

Morris observed that this opportunity to be part of creating something from the ground up helped them feel invested in it and connected: "We created it and made it what we needed." The new congregation, because of its size, also evoked in both Morris and Tonya the desire to be more real about their faith. There was no point in pretending since everyone knew what was going on in one another's lives anyway. Tonya describes being deeply moved when she considers the quiet, ongoing investment of people from the congregation who enact God's love and grace in the community. Morris describes how the church provides a regular centering time for him. For Tonya and Morris, finding a place in a congregation in their young adulthood took a detour that led them to an even deeper commitment to living their faith. Finding a place meant creating a place with enough theological breathing room.[8]

For most of those with whom I spoke, a period of fallowness with regard to church involvement was a reality, whether to allow time to cleanse the palate from bad church experiences or to give opportunity for an adult sense of agency to grow stronger in their spirits. I like Maggie's words to describe the way the transition time functioned in her life: "Without stepping away, without leaving the church for a while, I would not have ended up in the church with which I feel so pleased."[9]

Making Sense of Faithful Fallowness

When the individuals I interviewed spoke of a fallow period, it was typically during the period now termed "emerging adulthood," which begins around age eighteen and can continue through the mid- to late-twenties, depending on the person. It makes sense to me that commitments of their families of origin, largely influenced by their parents' authority and values, would be reevaluated once young people begin building their own lives in newly emancipated adulthood. Newly aware that the work of composing their own meaning-making structures now falls within their purview, it seems logical that young adults would begin to put their new critical awareness skills to use.

Sociologist Jeffrey Jensen Arnett describes three pillars of identity that emerging adults are in the process of composing: love, work, and ideology. The meaning of his categories of love and work are fairly self-evident. Ideology has to do with one's worldview, with how a person makes sense of the world. This almost universally has to do with religious beliefs and values.[10]

Sharon Parks would have us understand that people during this stage are moving from an authority-bound worldview or ideology to one they have themselves composed and given authority.[11] Arnett's study agrees but goes a step further, exposing an exaggeration of the emerging adults' need to assemble their own lives. His study illustrates a sense of failure the emerging adults feared they would have felt if they had merely continued the religious practices of their parents rather than critically reasoning every aspect of their beliefs and values for themselves. Arnett muses about the findings of his research that childhood religious training seems to have little to do with how emerging adults will compose meaning during this period. He does observe that, when exploring the role emerging adults anticipate religious training will play in the lives of their children, many do intend to include some sort of religious experience in their upbringing.[12] This perhaps reflects a vestige of tacit respect for their parents' beliefs and values and the benefits they received as a result. Whatever the case, a period of fallowness with regard to active engagement in a congregation seems to be a reality for many emerging adults.

In using the term *faithful fallowness* for this experience of being away from active engagement with a congregation for a time, I mean to indicate the evidence that young adults are indeed engaged in meaning-making work with regard to their beliefs and values during this period. Much was going on inside them; it just wasn't always evident on the outside, nor would it have been evident to those who didn't know them well and understand their lives. The example from Cathy's life, where she needed to get some distance from the toxic aspects of her religious upbringing, sheds light on one possible reason for apparent inactivity. Bill's story about floundering in frustration at injustice, which led to depression, which finally abated when he found his voice and vocation through faith-based justice work, is another example of active engagement with faith issues on the inside that would otherwise look like inactivity to those on the outside. It seems, in many cases, apparent inactivity masks deep engagement and struggle for a faith of their own that blesses them.

When I use the phrase *faithful fallowness*, I also mean to reflect the paradox of this time in life. It may seem on the surface, as Arnett's research suggests, that emerging adults have no interest in faith or congregation

---

Paying attention means . . .

■ Developing real friendships with adolescents. Take the time to know them as people.

■ Keeping track of those adolescent friends as they grow through emerging adulthood. Do this in power-balanced, rather than top-down, ways.

■ Connect with these younger friends outside of church, much as you would with other grown-up church friends.

In practical terms, this means you might . . .

■ Attend the performances or activities of adolescents in your congregation.

■ Ask your younger friends about their work or school life. Treat them with the respect you would other grown-ups.

■ Share about your own life in ways that begin in ways other than, "When I was your age . . . ."

■ Recognize that your younger friends are more than just their age.

■ Respect the choices of younger friends to attend or not attend worship. Help them know you enjoy their company and insights when they do.

■ Keep in touch younger friends without making them feel you are "checking up" on them. "I missed catching up with you last week. How are things going?" is a good way to start.

---

involvement, or that they have abandoned belief altogether.[13] My interviews seem to indicate that there are many reasons why emerging and young adults find it necessary to become less active in a local congregation. To judge them for their absence without understanding it is both unfair and unkind. Their need to feel that the community of faith is supporting them in their quests for meaning during this period is perhaps deeper than ever—whether they show up on Sundays for worship or not.

In his book *Souls in Transition*, Christian Smith draws the following conclusion about congregations' practices regarding emerging adults: "If communities of other adults . . . care about youth [and] wish to nurture emerging adult lives of purpose, meaning, and character—instead of confusion, drifting, and shallowness—they will need to do better jobs of seriously engaging youth from early on and not cut them adrift as they move through the teenage years."[14]

The stories of young adults I interviewed sometimes tell of individual members of faith communities from earlier in their lives who tethered them to their faith through their emerging adult years, but it seems to have been rarer to have entire communities of faith who remained in relationship with them when those emerging adults seemed disinterested. It is almost as if faith communities "rejected them back" when they felt like emerging adults were rejecting them.

Notes

1. Author interview recording with Cathy, September 17, 2009, around minute 19 and between minutes 59 and 67.

2. Author interview recording with Holly and Kraig, September 5, 2009, around minute 58.

3. Ibid., between minutes 38 and 52.

4. Ibid., between minutes 62 and 101.

5. Author interview recording with Andie, September 2, 2009, between minutes 46 and 60.

6. Author interview recording with Laurie, September 4, 2009, between minutes 19 and 43.

7. Author interview recording with Dana, December 29, 2009, between minutes 20 and 53.

8. Author interview recording with Morris and Tonya, March 26, 2009, between minutes 70 and 99.

9. Author interview recording with Maggie, September 2, 2009, about minute 26.

10. Jeffrey Jensen Arnett, *Emerging Adulthood: The Winding Road from the Late Teens through the Twenties* (New York: Oxford University Press, 2004), 165–66.

11. Sharon Daloz Parks, *Big Questions, Worthy Dreams: Mentoring Young Adults in Their Search for Meaning, Purpose, and Faith* (San Francisco: Jossey-Bass, 2000), 71.

12. Arnett, *Emerging* Adulthood, 174–77.

13. Ibid., 174.

14. Christian Smith with Patricia Snell, *Souls in Transition: The Religious and Spiritual Lives of Emerging Adults* (New York: Oxford University Press, 2009), 299.

PART THREE

MAKING WAY

Larry took very seriously his congregation's teaching about sharing his faith with others. As a young adult working at a music store, he had plenty of opportunities to reach out to local musicians. Larry developed a friendship with one of these musicians named Steve by offering a listening ear when Steve was feeling especially depressed and lost. Larry even went with his friends to a few of Steve's gigs. Eventually Steve decided to learn more about this Jesus whom Larry said helped him to have compassion for others. Steve showed up at church one Sunday, which was a big deal for him because he had played a gig the night before and didn't get home to bed until after 4:00 a.m. Steve missed worship but made it in time for Sunday school, still dressed in his clothes from the night before. Steve was greeted with some skeptical and scornful looks from church members who mistook him for an unwelcome vagrant—until Larry saw him and greeted Steve with a big hug. Larry was so excited that his witness had worked, only to see the looks of derision on the faces of the grown-ups, the same grown-ups who taught him to share his faith but left out an important caveat: "with the right kind of people."

* * *

Zach and his friends in the youth group had been working with their new youth pastor to plan a summer mission trip to Appalachia. Zach and his friends had been learning about the systemic poverty of

Appalachia at school and worked with their youth pastor to do a Bible study to help them figure out how they could respond to this injustice as people of faith. They didn't know how they would raise the several thousand dollars it would take for them to go; they certainly didn't have the money themselves. They went with their youth pastor to a meeting of the administrative board at their church to ask for help. Members of the administrative board were so moved by the young people's passion for justice and desire for the mission trip that they organized a rummage sale of members' and their friends' gently used stuff and raised all the money Zach and his friends needed for the mission trip, plus a nice head start on funding future trips. The youth were so transformed by the experience that they convinced the church to offer service learning trips for adults, often led by the passionate younger members. No one has ever had to pay his or her own way.

8

Beyond Silly Games, Thin Theology, and Serving Soup

A Word for Youth Ministry

Sometimes I feel like I'm the least faithful person in the room. . . . I just know God is good and God's grace is enough. —Maggie (study participant)

Youth ministry stereotypes are rampant in congregations—sometimes because the stereotype was the lived experience of some adults when they were youth. You probably don't have to think very hard to come up with them: choruses of "Kumbaya" around the campfire, silly games and gimmicky Bible studies, serving at the local soup kitchen without deeper reflection, a hip guitar-playing youth pastor who isn't much older than the youth in the youth group, a trip to camp or a regional youth gathering, or maybe a summer mission trip—these stereotypes and many more like them are unfortunately the reality in some congregations' youth ministries. It's unfortunate because, while they keep youth occupied (the first purpose of youth ministry historically), they aren't transformational and they don't provide much of a foundation for adult lives of faith. Fortunately, there are also lots of good youth ministry models out there that are transformational. I shared some of them in chapter two.

One such strategy is to begin to shape forms of knowing, dependence, and belonging in youth ministry. Dori Baker and Joyce Ann Mercer offer helpful insights about why and how to do this in their book *Lives to Offer*. They refer to James Fowler's statement about the myth in our culture that people are self-sufficient to create for themselves a "fulfilled and self-actualized life."[1] Christian faith offers a helpful corrective: "In our call *God* rewrites our lives; that we have new lives formed and reformed as the story of Christ begins to take shape in us."[2]

What a powerful way to help youth prepare for the work of emerging and young adulthood: understanding the work of assembling forms of knowing, dependence, and belonging that is beginning already and also lies ahead as a communal act! If vocation is a call to "partnership with God on behalf of neighbor,"[3] then vocation is not a solitary goal reflecting our own achievement, as our culture might lead us to believe. Vocation is rather a cooperative endeavor with God. Its purpose is not self-fulfillment alone but the good of neighbor and, I would add, the whole creation.

A colleague shared an insightful story about the youth ministry at her mainline Protestant congregation. A former youth ministry volunteer lamented what she saw as the fail point of the congregation's seemingly successful youth ministry program in previous years. The volunteer referred to the program as "seemingly successful" because several youth were involved and they did a lot of activities, but they weren't very transformative and many wandered away from the church in the transition from youth to young adulthood. The former volunteer confessed that while the program of the earlier era involved many of the same aspects as the current program, at least one key difference emerged. As this former volunteer reflected on it, the difference that positively impacted the transition of youth from youth group into active engagement in congregations in that context is that their experience in youth ministry now gives them the theological vocabulary for the otherwise good activities it has undertaken all along.

Youth ministry at its best provides space for youth to ask big enough questions, as Sharon Parks terms them. Youth ministry helps adolescents explore vocation as they begin to assemble meaning in their lives for themselves. My conversation partners in the academic field of youth ministry each use their own language to talk around the topic of vocation and meaning-making with adolescents and young adults. They speak of passion and idealism and curiosity and energy as qualities of adolescents. They note the need for youth ministry to connect all of those qualities with faith. They observe the roles of parents and other adults in the lives of youth, referring to them without necessarily naming the ideas of scaffolding or mentoring. I don't disagree, but I think youth and young adults deserve more from their communities of faith.

If the National Study of Youth and Religion that I wrote about earlier in this work accurately depicts adolescents as inarticulate about their faith, then we might deduce that youth need tools and models to better articulate their faith. Or, because articulateness is not an end in itself, perhaps what youth really need is more of the transformation that leads to articulateness among other things in the first place. Another way of identifying transformation beyond articulateness is to observe evidence of it in life patterns and choices. However we identify it, transformation is key to effectiveness in ministry of any type, including youth ministry. One purpose of this study was to identify aspects of youth ministry that were particularly transformative as identified by grown-ups who experienced transformation in youth ministry as evidenced in their active engagement in congregations as young adults.

Before we move on to consider what we heard from those young adults, we need to deal with one more issue first. I believe a key hurdle congregations need to overcome in ministry with adolescents and young adults involves the transition from adolescence to adulthood in the church's programming. Youth ministry has done a pretty good job of seeing itself in continuity with what comes before—with ministry with children—more so than it has understood itself in continuity with what comes next—adult developmental steps and adult engagement in a community of faith. My study reflects the need for a corrective in this area, to more intentionally focus on the transition from adolescence through emerging adulthood to young adulthood, all within the context of helping youth make this transition within the community of faith to the greatest extent possible. Again, paying attention is key.

A Deeper Look at Transformational Youth Ministry

This project began with a question: What about the adolescent church experience of currently church-active twenty- and thirty-somethings might have led them into active engagement with a congregation in these young adult years? After all, everyone knows that the so-called millennials are among the "missing generations" in local congregations across the nation. I say here that millennials are *among* the mission generations because gradually since the 1950s the ratio of members of generations "missing" from congregations has grown, but the idea of missing generations is far from new. This leads us to ask: What could have created these notable exceptions to the growing norm? What allowed these young adults to escape the "epidemic" that created the nones and the dones?

Paying Attention in Youth Ministry

We can discover important insights for youth ministry today by revisiting the key factors already identified by my young adult interviewees, things that made their teenage experiences in church memorable, sustainable, and redeemable. Remember that we grouped those factors under four headings: identity entanglements, still small voices and vocations, the sacramentality of real relationships, and faithful fallowness and the way back home.

Young adults highlighted what I called *identity entanglements*—describing how the central role of faith and faith community in their teen years shaped their essential identities, their emerging sense of self. This dynamic suggests that a deep sense of having their identity "all tangled up" with faith and the church provided a tether to help young adults find their way back home to a community of faith.

Based on my interviews, one key way congregations can foster an environment where youth understand aspects of their identity as comingled with faith and faith communities is to create an environment where exploration is central, where questioning is welcomed, and where there is more than one right answer. Early on, when they are still children and younger youth, foster an environment of wondering aloud together. Asking questions together about what a particular story from the Bible might mean rather than giving only one interpretation of it gives younger people a sense of the expansiveness of God and the creativity God employs in God's interaction with humanity.

Take their questions seriously. Adolescence is a time for questioning everything! Socrates is credited with positing that he could not teach anybody anything but rather only make them think. Adolescents need adults who can deal with their questioning and help those adolescents think things through, leading them gently in learning for themselves. Congregations help form faith identity when they take seriously the integration of faith questions and life experiences to assist youth as well as grown-ups in their ongoing meaning-making at every life stage. This study indicates that the faithfulness of grown-ups in congregations matters in the lives of youth, even if they have little to no direct contact with youth.

Additionally, a strong faith identity is fostered when we provide language for youth (and even children) to express where and how they see God at work in the world and in their lives—even as we recognize that their understanding will continue to grow as they do. Commit to using that language along with them to help them practice and reinforce the concept.

Fostering a group identity among youth as well as part of the larger congregation is integral to formation of identity as part of a larger body of people who are also living faithfully. Give youth times to be together with others their age as well as opportunities to interact across the life cycle with others who share their gifts and passions. Both are critical.

Finally, congregations can help foster a sense of growing investment in the faith community by involving youth (and older children) meaningfully in the life of the congregation in ways that use their *gifts*. This means going beyond grouping children or youth by age when considering how to involve them, and it means going beyond token involvement ("cuteness") to doing something real and meaningful. This leads us to the next insight we gained from those interviews.

Many young adults shared stories of finding their *voice* and discerning their *vocation* through significant church experiences that fostered their faith. Opportunities to testify to their faith with their words and actions inspired them and helped them create meaning and depth that sustained them through hypocrisy and disappointment with their congregations. The idea that God needs us to do something important in the world has the power to capture imaginations and to sustain young people's commitment to the faith community—because they can imagine a place for themselves in that community.

Service to others can provide a sense of voice and vocation when it is integrated into the congregation's life and when experiences are tied to reflection on deeper issues of justice. Youth (and adults) can find meaningful expression for their passion and gifts in service, but service that simply "does good" without theological reflection on the deeper issues dilutes the impact. Connecting their personal passions with the injustices and needs of the larger world can be a critical aspect of identity formation for youth.

Further, opportunities for youth to learn to use their emerging sense of voice is also key. This can be through service on committees and task forces, but such service needs to be real and not token. A committee that creates no space for an adolescent to speak or one that squelches their ideas or questions defeats the purpose. Worse, a committee that discusses a topic and then turns to the teenage member to ask what "the youth" think about the topic uses tokenism to teach the teenage member implicitly that she is nothing more than her age and that her own considered opinions don't matter. Giving youth and young adults space to learn to speak up, to share ideas, to think critically and theologically, and to question is vital to adolescents' emerging sense of voice and vocation.

Specifically, this means that grown-ups in congregations need to be challenged to set aside self-interest and make space for youth to find voice and vocation. Plainly put, this means grown-ups need to grow up and get over themselves, and let go of the church as a vehicle for meeting their need for self-importance. Perfect programs and well-managed budgets matter little if the next generation does not find a place in the community of faith or a reason to be there. By holding on too tightly in a variety of unhelpful ways, adults sometimes strangle to death the church they claim to love.

Voice and vocation were "handles" for some of the participants in my study to find their way back to church as young adults. But things like community service and mission trips alone do not necessarily create the kinds of handles they need, as echoed by experts in the field. Youth need interpreters and companions and mentors nearby—they need a congregation of faithful disciples modeling for them by giving voice to their faith and living their vocation as fully as possible every day.[4]

The stories I heard throughout my interviews made it clear: *relationships* matter to adolescents and young adults. But not just any relationship is transformational. I heard in my interviews that youth experience *authentic* relationships as being almost sacramental—transmitting *tangible grace*. My interviewees cherished grown-ups who remained genuine with them, who demonstrated integrity in their own faith, who walked alongside as the teens developed their own ways to make meaning of life. Young adults told me in various ways that "being there" matters, and the quality of that presence matters too.

What do I (and they) mean by "quality" in grown-up presence? Youth and young adults seem almost allergic to any hint of injustice and incongruence (what they often call hypocrisy) in people. Considering typical patterns of human development, this makes sense at their place in life. Of course, we all struggle daily to align our practices with what we say we believe. Eventually, most of us realize that we all need a little grace because none of us is completely consistent in living out our convictions. Because young people haven't yet developed tools to deal with their own hypocrisy, much less the hypocrisy of older and more powerful adults (who should know better, and therefore *be better*), youth and young adults respect and value a community of faith that deals honestly with its shortcomings and strives to live into to its convictions. So, if the bread of relational communion is "being there," then the cup is filled with the fruit of our lived faith. As younger generations have put it, "being real" is an integral part of "being there."

More than just being real, this project amplifies the calls of others in the field of youth ministry for less incongruity between youth and adult programming. The disjuncture in the transition from youth ministry to being a regular adult member is often problematic for young adults who suddenly find themselves on foreign turf in communities of faith. What I'm talking about here is a kind of continuity between what it means to be an adolescent in the church and what it means to be an adult—a continuity that invites youth into the adult congregation in developmentally appropriate ways that ease the transition into adult roles.

When the primary point of connection with the congregation has been through the youth minister or sponsors, young adults can find themselves lost and adrift in their own congregations. Beginning to make connections with grown-ups around areas of passion and vocation in teen years can help minimize this disruption for young adults. Working alongside others on a Habitat for Humanity build, or painting the backdrops for Vacation Bible School alongside grown-ups with similar gifts, can both demonstrate respect for the real gifts youth offer and create tethering relationships of continuing connection. Worship that occasionally incorporates music and other elements youth may have experienced to be powerful when attending camps or conferences can provide an important point of connection for adolescents and young adults. This may require some getting used to on the part of older members, but a gentle reminder that worship planning requires taking into account the needs of the whole worshipping community often reassures those who might bristle that their needs, too, are important and will be taken into account, as well.

Rites of passage can help. A rite of passage can be as simple as formally acknowledging that an adolescent has reached the age of majority (also the age of full membership in some congregations) by consciously beginning to relate to the emerging adult directly rather than through their parents. Create separate entries in the church directory for all newly minted adults, even if they are still living with parents. Give them their own offering envelopes, pledge cards, and giving statements (but don't let that be the only rite of passage since it could be misinterpreted). Invite them personally into leadership and service rather than sending messages through parents.

More formal rituals are already part of this transition to adulthood in some cultures. Many African American congregations use programs like Young Lions or Daughters of Imani as ways to formalize movement into adulthood—an act that benefits both the adolescent and the grown-ups in the congregation by what is being observed in the change that is taking place.

Finally, young adults related stories of *faith* during apparently *fallow* periods in their lives—seasons when they disengaged from faith communities. Their stories reveal a depth of faith and struggle in this time away. Far from a lack of faith, emerging adults described a journey of healing or discovery in their faith identity, as they explored new understandings of authority, dependence, and belonging to undergird their faith. For many of these young adults, the fallow period became a way back home, especially for those for whom church had always been "like family."

Youth and young adults benefit tremendously from staying connected with faith communities when experiencing a fallow period, particularly if they have had a long-term relationship with the church. When emerging adults need space and time away from congregational involvement—and this happens for a wide variety of reasons—congregations need to remain constant in their lives instead of "rejecting them back" when it feels like emerging adults are rejecting the church. The critical importance of "tethering" individuals and experiences in the lives of youth and young adults cannot be overstated. In practice, grown-up members who have had relationships with these younger adults can simply continue "checking in" with them, talking by phone or texting, staying connected through social media, sending care packages if they are living away from home, and meeting for coffee or lunch when that's the kind of relationship they've had with the younger adult. Authenticity is critical here again. As one of my study participants intimated, if the church has loved and cared for these younger adults when they were growing up, it would be very odd for the same group of people just to ignore a younger adult when he is "taking a break" from church, for whatever reason. Remaining connected—tethering—provides a supportive connection with a group of caring grown-ups while the younger adult sorts things out for himself.

Youth ministry is ever evolving, but that does not mean the practiced habits of youth ministry in congregations necessarily change much at all with each new era. I have gleaned some potentially helpful insights from my conversations with young adults that need to be shared widely among the actual practitioners of youth ministry. For me, writing a book that is read in universities and seminaries is not the most useful way to share these ideas. This and other promising research must speak to the church and evoke deep reflection about the future we hope to leave for our children's children.

Notes

1. James Fowler, *Becoming Adult, Becoming Christian: Adult Development and Christian Faith* (San Francisco: Harper & Row, 1984), 101–2.

2. Dori Grinenko Baker and Joyce Ann Mercer, *Lives to Offer: Accompanying Youth on Their Vocational Quests* (Cleveland, OH: Pilgrim, 2007), 162–63.

3. Fowler, *Becoming Adult, Becoming Christian*, 102.

4. Christian Smith with Patricia Snell, *Souls in Transition: The Religious and Spiritual Lives of Emerging Adults* (New York: Oxford University Press, 2009), 254; Margaret Ann Crain, "Staying Awake," in Dori Grinenko Baker, ed., *Greenhouses of Hope: Congregations Growing Young Leaders Who Will Change the World* (Herndon, VA: Alban Institute, 2010), 47.

9

Making Space for Faithful Following
A Word for Not-So-Young Adults

As people live longer and are healthy and active further into older adulthood, a logjam of sorts is created. Older adults who have found great meaning—perhaps sometimes too great—in their congregational roles over the years are reluctant to step back from those roles. Sometimes holding on to those roles becomes a way of denying the effects of aging or the coming end of life, while other times these dear friends simply may have mistaken the goal of congregational decision making as doing things "right" when the goal is better understood as doing things faithfully.

Too frequently this logjam sends messages to younger adults that they are not needed or there is no room for them. For young adults full of fresh ideas, eager to use their newly found voices and invest themselves in the vocations to which they feel called, the logjam can be painful and defeating. Solutions such as invitations to serve on "junior" boards or as children's church volunteers do not satisfy many of these young adults, whose real passion lies in changing the world through justice ministries, righting the wrongs they see with sharp precision at their place in life.

Something is broken in our congregations. A paradigm shift is required. Let's look at a couple of ways to think differently about the church's logjam.

The "Already Committed" Have the
Privilege of Making Space

My Baha'i friends tell me that only Baha'is have the privilege of supporting Baha'i houses of worship and other work with their time, talent, and
treasure. It is understood to be an honor, as a member of the Baha'i faith,
to contribute one's resources—whether great or small—to the construc-
tion of beautiful houses of worship, one on each continent, that inspire
people of all faiths with their glorious architecture and harmonious
design. Only Baha'is—those already convinced and involved in Baha'i
meetings and the work of ministry—have the opportunity to enact that
faith and give freely of their resources so that others who are searching
might find hospitable space in the Baha'i houses of worship. Consider
the wisdom of this way of thinking: those who are already committed to
the faith take responsibility for giving of themselves to make space for
those not yet convinced to seek God.

I see parallels in this principle for how grown-ups in the church might
better understand their role with regard to making space for emerging
and young adults in communities of faith. What if our paradigm shifted
from one of *ownership*, where the desire to control reigns, to one of
stewardship, where the passion to share is encouraged? Those with
power and privilege presently often learned from their forebears in the
faith some patterns of behavior that are less than helpful.

When I observe the way elders sometimes teach and foster bullying
through their behaviors, it makes me curious about how they were treated as young adults. I wonder if they were full of ideas and energy and were
forced to give in to their elders on worship style and other church matters.
While not explicitly expressed, actions sometimes belie a retributive "now
it's my time to get my way" kind of bullying of elders toward younger
adults, which is not only unfaithful but becomes a vicious cycle of bullying—a cycle that needs to be broken with intentionality.

How much more life-giving and meaningful, both for established
grown-ups and for younger adults and youth, if elders used their power
and privilege intentionally to make space for others whose voices are not
as established: "I'm already committed to faith. Now, as an elder mem-

ber, I have the privilege of making space for emerging and young adults in the faith community." Truly all people can use their power to serve only their own needs. That's scarcity thinking.

What if we paid attention to the abundance all around us instead of scratching and clawing to have our own needs met? There's plenty of space in the family of faith for everyone. Making room for others is the privilege of those already convinced! Making space for youth and young adults, and for all those not yet invested in living the gospel, is the privilege of those who are strengthened by the love of God and the communion of the saints!

Paying attention means ...

■ Expecting older adults to care about the church thriving beyond their own lifetimes.

■ Trusting the God of our foremothers and forefathers to continue gifting the next generations, too.

■ Carefully discerning the difference between personal preferences and matters of faith.

■ Recognizing the value in the traditions of elders and reclaiming life-giving aspects in the midst of new practices.

In practical terms, this means you might ...

■ Decide it's better to adapt your worship to use language that helps those new to faith learn and grow.

■ Set aside your own preferences about technology in worship to better embrace the preferences of those whose expectations differ.

■ Get to know and love those whose opinions differ; doing so will help you want their needs to be met, too.

■ Love others in the congregation with a 1 Corinthians 13 kind of love (patient and kind, etc.).

■ Offer yourself some grace when you feel discomfort with non-preferred ways of doing things; extend the same grace to others when they may feel out-of-sorts.

So, What Do We Mean by "Making Space"?

This chapter began with a fact of postmodern life—people are living longer with many more productive years of life than previous generations, resulting in a logjam of leadership in congregations. Making space involves ensuring opportunities for younger adults to exercise their gifts and leadership as part of a healthy mix of generations involved in decision making in the life of the church. I refer to this practice as "making space" because many younger adults honor their elders as sacred. This is particularly true in African American, Hispanic, and Asian cultures, and it is reflected in congregations where people of these cultures dominate the membership.

A young adult student in a course I teach put it this way: "I was raised that way [to honor elders] and it almost seems unchristian to think of questioning what they say." However, honoring elders unquestioningly—whether or not that honor is earned—can actually be unhelpful to children, youth, and younger adults. An obvious example is the way unquestioning respect of elders can give those who might abuse children a foothold to keep those children from questioning and refusing inappropriate behavior. More subtly for youth and young adults, being trained to honor all older adults can equate to a reticence in claiming their own emerging adult voices. They have questions and hunches emerging inside them, which they need to speak aloud and act on in order to grow into their adult selves. And older adults in the church need to make space—physical, spiritual, and psychological space—for those emerging voices to be heard.

A Deeper Look at Older Adults Making Space

Fern's Story

While serving as a major gifts officer for the development office of a seminary some years ago, I met an elderly woman named Fern. My job was to ask Fern for a gift to increase her scholarship fund at the school—money we received faithfully and annually—but Fern loved to tell stories, so my encounter with her became so much more than a typical "ask."

In between wanting to hear what was going on at the seminary, Fern invited me to help her think through what she believed God was calling her to do. Lately she had been thinking a lot about the dozens of children she noticed outside playing when she was on her way to Sunday worship at her local church—children she believed needed the benefits of a loving church family and Sunday school. She told me about the mobile home park on the edge of town where she saw the kids, a place often referred to as an eyesore by townsfolk in her small Iowa hamlet. The man who owned it, Bob, was called a slum landlord by those townsfolk who wanted the place "cleaned up."

Fern remembered Bob as a student in her children's Sunday school class years ago. She told me she knew in her heart that Bob was not a bad guy. So Fern went to Bob and asked if she could start a Sunday school at the trailer park. Bob, now a gruff and distrustful man, agreed to the idea, but he wondered what she was going to do when it rained since the program was to be held outdoors. Fern told him not to worry, that they would figure it out. It turns out that it hasn't rained at the time of the program since they started meeting, now many years ago. Fern learned, through the families of the Sunday school children, that Bob is actually a generous landlord, allowing many undocumented immigrant inhabitants of the trailer park to move in without paying if they do not have the money, and permitting them to pay when they can as they get settled and have income.

Over the years, I visited Fern at least annually, and her story unfolded with each visit. Fern discovered that many children from the trailer park and throughout the town came from families that did not have money for school supplies and backpacks, so she and some other women started a back-to-school giveaway. Then they formed a foundation to provide these kinds of things for the children of the county. They fund aquatic center memberships annually for hundreds of families who otherwise would not be able to afford to use the city's new public pool. They provide prom dresses and activity fee scholarships for many more students to participate in typical high school activities. In small and inglorious ways, they try to help their neighbors, following Jesus' example.

Fern also decided that she knew many people whose lives were inspiring to her in quiet, simple ways—ways that probably nobody realized. This spurred her to interview members of the community and retell their stories in a series of books she self-published. People like Bob, the trailer park owner, and many others whose good deeds went unnoticed were featured in these books. For Fern, there is something sacred in the story of almost every person she meets; her stories lift up the child of God in each.

Fern, aged ninety-six at the time of a newspaper article about her in the *Des Moines Register in* August of 2011,[1] is a woman who lives her faith, who is paying attention, who has skin in the game, who is awake and alert for the possible ways of living her vocation that are all around her. She probably prays and reads the Bible daily, and she is generous with her resources and her time. Christian practices are a regular part of her life. But there is something more going on with Fern, something I think of as living her faith. It likely is not even a conscious thing for her anymore. It is simply who she is.

Fern's story illustrates the difference between being a Christian and living life as a transformed disciple of Jesus Christ. More importantly, I tell Fern's story to lift up the kind of older adult that young adults need.

To begin with, Fern lives out her faith in ways that have cost her reputation capital in her small Iowa town. More than that, Fern realized in her early sixties that she had held nearly every position in the church, including judicatory and denominational elected positions. She had proven to herself and others that she could do it all—that wasn't the point for her anymore. She discerned that it was time for her to foster the leadership of others in her local church, to support them heartily.

Fern understood that her God-given vocation and gifts didn't expire when she "retired" from church leadership positions. She saw the freedom and time she now had as a gift—one that she needed to use to continue to help others in new ways. The second half of her life turned out to be as rich with possibility as the first had been but in different ways. Her ministry at the trailer park and the books of biographies she published were a continuation of her leadership and vision. While she made space for younger leaders to serve within their giftedness, she also made space for herself to continue to follow God faithfully in new ways in a new phase of life.

Rethinking What It Means to Be a Respected Elder

Author and scholar Parker Palmer, now in his seventies, reframes a dominant question emerging in older adulthood in this way: To what shall I give myself? As we age, no longer can we accomplish all we once did or do everything we have always done, just because. Palmer discerned that he didn't so much need to hang on to some things in his life as he aged. Hanging on, he came to understand, was a needy and fearful posture in relation to things he has or does. Rather, as he considers letting go of things in his life, he now asks himself, "To what shall I give myself?" He finds it helps him choose whether or not to say yes to an investment of his limited mental and physical energy. His posture is one of sharing the resource that is his life generously and also wisely. Might older adults in the congregation find greater meaning as they come to see themselves as investing in the lives of the younger adults and youth in their midst? Could this way of reframing their identities in the congregation open up new meaning while also creating space for younger voices and visions?[2]

For example, an older adult might decide that he no longer needs to be in charge of a particular ministry at church but will intentionally remain involved to support the incoming younger adult leader in her role. With the respect the older adult has earned over many years of faithful service, he will offer words of encouragement to the new leader. Rather than receive the changes the new leader makes as a personal affront, the older adult will reflect openly and nonjudgmentally with the new leader, identifying and celebrating positive aspects and perhaps reserving critical comments, offering them privately and infrequently with the new leader when invited. The older adult could also choose to use his considerable influence to become the informal "positive press agent" for the new leader, talking up her strengths. In this way, the older adult would bless the new leader rather than curse her with his words and actions.

Judy had a growing sense of concern about the quantity of waste the congregation was generating through weekly coffee hours and potluck dinners. At a Women's Club meeting a few months back, she heard some of her middle-aged friends complaining about the mess of trash bags around the dumpster as they entered. One of her friends blamed the custodian while another opined that perhaps they needed a larger dumpster. Judy herself felt the real solution was to reduce the amount of waste, but she kept her thoughts to herself.

At coffee hour the next week, she overheard some of the younger members discussing a similar concern for the waste, putting it in terms of environmental justice. Judy apologized for eavesdropping and asked if they had any ideas for addressing the issue. Judy and her new younger adult friends helped the congregation reduce its waste through a combination of recycling and offering people the option of reusable mugs and dishes at church events. The new Creation Care team, led by a younger adult who teamed up with Judy, hopes to start composting in a forgotten corner of the church property. They are working with their local garden club to make the compost available for the community garden next summer. A member of the garden club was excited to learn that the church cared about the environment, a long-time passion of hers, and has begun attending worship at the church.

Sankofa and a Word for Younger Adults

The Ghanaian image and proverb of *sankofa* offer another helpful paradigm shift for our consideration, particularly for young adults. African American scholar Jeffery Tribble, in his chapter "Embodying Sankofa" in *Greenhouses of Hope*, lifts up the idea of *sankofa*, "Go back and get it." Tribble describes a congregation that blesses its young adults with this image—a mythical bird flying forward with an egg in its mouth while looking backward—and the encouragement to "go back and get it" in the midst of exploring their own giftedness in the nurturing environment of the church. The egg of the *sankofa* image is said to represent both the treasured wisdom of those who have gone before *and* the treasure of the next generation who will benefit from the wisdom. In the image of the *sankofa* bird, it is by the bird's own initiative that it "goes back and gets it (that which it has lost or forgotten)." The bird chooses to go back; it is not forced. Young adults might hear this as encouragement to choose and seek that which is valuable in the heritage and legacy of those who have gone before, realizing that the treasure they seek is both within them and in the collective wisdom of the ancestors.

For young adults who seek the wisdom of the past while confidently flying forward into the future, *sankofa* can become a life-giving and

Marion retired to an area near her children and found herself, at nearly eighty, searching for a new congregation. At coffee with a friend, she bemoaned the way congregations seemed to assume, because she moved more slowly and had gray hair, that she held conservative values and resisted change. Marion loved change and new experiences, and she loved to be around younger folk. Their ideas were invigorating to her and their energy was contagious. In young people, she intimated, she found joy and hope. Marion died several years later and before she found a congregation where she had access to life-affirming younger people with whom she could learn and be inspired.

empowering concept. For older adults who are patient and honest as young adults develop the desire to seek their heritage and discern the wisdom from it, retelling and relearning the legacy can be liberating, as well.

In Tribble's chapter, he tells the story of a twenty-nine-year-old young man, a relatively new member at First African Church in Lithonia, Georgia, who chairs the congregation's board of trustees. The young man is a wealth manager, a business owner, and an investor who understands part of his personal call to be developing distressed properties into safe housing for single-parent families. The pastor lifted him up as a gifted leader and placed him in this position as chair of the trustees, and the congregation (including older adults) embraced his leadership and supported his growth intentionally, recognizing that vocation and giftedness are not bound by age, and that the church needs courageous and energetic leaders today like the apostles of the early church. It took intentionality on the part of this congregation to step outside of the church's traditional pattern of promoting people into leadership through a series of increasingly responsible positions. It took paying attention.[3]

Notes

1. Paula Reece, "An Osceola Powerhouse," *Des Moines Register*, August 15, 2011.

2. Krista Tippett, *On Being*, November 12, 2014, www.onbeing.org/blog/the-choice-of-hanging-on-or-giving-to/7029.

3. Jeffery Tribble, "Embodying Sankofa," in *Greenhouses of Hope*, ed. Dori Grinenko Baker (Herndon, VA: Alban Institute, 2010), 140, 154–55.

10

A Faith to *Live* For

A Word for Young Adults and Youth

Congregations sometimes seek young adult members as if their acquisition somehow validates those congregations' existence. Doing so causes those congregations to lose sight of the ultimate goal, which is to minister to and with these beloved children of God who happen to be chronologically younger. Even good people, who are lifelong members of congregations, sometimes behave in ways that are paradoxical. Congregations say they want to attract young adult members but then do the things we all know just aren't very kind: some assume they know what young adults need or want without asking; some expect younger adults to submit to the preferences and demands of their elders without question; some expect young adults to start at the bottom of the church ladder and work their way up. Churches know better than to behave in these ways, but they still do sometimes.

I found an example of such inhospitable behavior in the book *Tribal Church* by Carol Howard Merritt, where she tells of her husband, Brian's, experience as a church consultant, drawing on another author's term for young adults in the church: *Survivors*. The story goes like this:

> [Brian] introduced the term [Survivors], took a deep breath, and braced himself as if he were driving into a predicted storm. Sure enough, the sky began to thunder as the familiar outrage began. "Survivors? Did you say 'Survivors'? What have they had to survive?"

"They didn't have World War II or Vietnam."

"They didn't go through the civil rights movement."

"They're recipients of unprecedented wealth!"

"I open up the real estate ads, and I can't believe how much these people will pay for a house!"

"They are so materialistic."

"You know, my nephew is still living with his parents. He's twenty-five years old."

Brian typically keeps his mouth closed during these long rants. When the storm subsides, he gently explains, "We're called Survivors because we've had to survive years of being treated like this."[1]

Whether older church members actually say these things out loud or just use them to inform their behavior, insights like this help us understand what it can be like for young adults to take their first hesitant steps back toward a community of faith. It seems the people who think or say these things forget their own transition to adulthood in a congregation, or perhaps they had less-than-helpful models in the way they were welcomed. It really doesn't matter why it happens.

The tricky part is this: when not-so-young adults say these things or even think them, they reflect a pain from their own lives that needs healing. Many times people who say these things heard them or felt judged unfairly as younger adults themselves. Those who have experienced deep hurts sometimes lash out at the very people for whom it might seem they should have the greatest empathy. This disjuncture may well be amplified by the different value systems that emerge as each generation is shaped by the experiences of their era. While those not-so-young adults long for youth and younger adults in their congregations, their unhealed woundedness sometimes leads to inhospitable behavior. Some might say, "Well, we had to put up with unfair things like assumptions and hierarchical rather than vocational calls to service," to which I'd offer the pastoral response, "You should not have had to. That behavior was hurtful and wrong and outside of the love to which our faith compels us." In a paradox like this, someone has to break the cycle. If the paradoxical cycle hasn't been broken to this point, then the future faithfulness of the congregation demands that each of us give our whole selves to this task.

A Faith to *Live* For

I made the claim in an earlier chapter that what youth and young adults are looking for—what their passion connects with most poignantly—is a faith that's worth living for. After all, adolescence can be a passionate time of life, full of energy and hope and possibilities and 'why not?' questions. Of course, it can also be an overwhelming and anxiety-ridden time of existential despair that can rob one of hope. A faith worth living for offers the hope and security that adolescence has failed to offer.

The life Jesus lived on earth was a passionate one throughout his brief years and was marked by the unquenchable hope fueled by a deep belief in one's mission. Jesus' life is one with which many youth and young adults connect in deep and life-giving ways. Consider how Jesus sided with the marginalized while not "kissing up" to power brokers for his own personal gain—this is a key way in which Jesus' passion for justice connects with the adolescent drive for fairness and authenticity. From Jesus' passion for healing and wholeness to the love he showed to the least, the last, the lost, the little ones, and the lonely, it is evident that Jesus was consciously engaged in living his faith. Even when challenged by older and more powerful religious authorities, Jesus seemed guided by his own internal sense of vocation and voice—another example that adolescents and young adults will connect with.

Authentic qualities such as these that Jesus exemplified throughout his life are things all of us, but particularly young adults, wish we more fully embodied. This passionately faithful life is intriguing and inspiring—it connects with the passionate part of each of us.

Youth and young adults need contexts that make space for them to explore how the passion they feel connects with the world's greatest need at an intersection often referred to as vocation. Local congregations can be a place for this exploration *inasmuch as they remain open to the questions and critique that youth and young adults uncover along their journey.*

For congregations that can manage the anxiety and discomfort that comes with this questioning and critiquing, the effect of youth and young adults' engagement is often life-affirming and generative. And for those congregations that cannot manage the possibility of change in healthy ways—particularly for the youth and young adults in those congregations—the process can be painful and disruptive. Too many youth and young adults find themselves de-churched because their questions were not welcome, and too many congregations scratch their heads in befuddlement at what just transpired.

Morris and Tonya experienced this as young adults emerging into leadership in the congregation where Morris had grown up. Tonya questioned curricular and programming choices for youth and children, recommending relational and transformational emphases rather than those that were didactic and rigid, but her questions were rejected out of hand. When her voice was squelched by those whose power mandated the changes, Tonya and Morris both soon found their church home to be inhospitable. They no longer felt like "their" church was for them. Tonya and Morris eventually settled at another church, a place they describe as enlivened with deep questions in the midst of deep and real relationships. Tonya values the openness to questions for herself and Morris but even more so now that she anticipates this environment for her children when they reach that stage of life.

One more thing: Tonya would be the first to say that when she was a younger adult she was still learning to speak up for herself, to use her growing sense of agency and voice. Sometimes, when she felt the most frustrated with the "powers that be" not listening to her, she was really frustrated with herself for not being able to make herself heard. Granted, some of it had to do with the disempowering actions of older adults, but it was also true that she simply wasn't very sure of herself yet—she wasn't very empowered. Another paradox emerges here when young adults use their emerging voices in the adult world and feel unheard. This is another time when paying attention more carefully and extending ample grace to one another goes a long way toward healing.

Healthy Congregations and Being Church

You may have gathered by now that it takes work—both within individuals and in the congregation as a group—to welcome and celebrate the giftedness of people throughout the life cycle. Sometimes it would seem easier for younger adults to consider starting a separate congregation or at least a separate worship service just for them. It might be easier, but so much richness would be lost. Vital congregations have a healthy mix of engaged participants across the life cycle. Churches need the gifts of each generation: the long view of history from older members, the energy and investment of midlife members, and the fresh perspectives and innovation of young adults.[2]

As we have observed before, many mainline churches see one or more generations missing from the mix. Soul-searching members ask where the young people are—not even noticing that many from their own age group are not in church either. The cynical among us may seek somewhere to place the blame, pointing to cultural distractions (e.g., intermural sports or other community activities scheduled on Sundays) or indicting the young adults themselves, deeming them self-centered and uncaring. But wouldn't a more faithful response be to look for signs of God's love and grace among young adults and then ask how the church might join in?

When congregations become prideful, thinking their programs and processes are finally perfected and no longer need to adapt or change, they squelch the new life they claim they want to see and they tell youth and young adults who are eager to invest, "Your gifts and insights are not needed here." When youth and young adults become impatient and seek to have all their ideas validated and adopted without critical discernment about continuity with the church's mission and vision, they devalue the good work that has been done by those who came before them. Neither is acceptable, because the church needs all those gifts.

I'm reminded of the conversation Jesus had with the disciples in which the disciples question Jesus about others who are healing in his name (Mark 9:38–41). They proudly announced their efforts to stop the activity because the healers were not part of their group. Jesus' response, "Whoever is not against us is for us," provides the following insight: those doing the work of love and justice are partners in God's work in the world alongside churches.

Let me share with you the stories of some twentysomethings who found ways to live out their God-given vocations in creative ways largely outside the church through their social service, social justice, and advocacy work. Those interviewed[3] in this round of investigations were all actively engaged in mainline congregations as adolescents, but most are not presently active in church. In these young adults, I found passionate people engaged in acts of love and justice through their vocations, friendships, and communities. These stories are prime examples of Jesus' teaching about those not being against us actually being for us.

■ Judy went to law school intending to work in criminal prosecution or defense because she wanted to work for justice for those without a voice. Instead, she found herself drawn to bankruptcy law. In her work, she listens to people who are at the end of their ropes—people who have been taken advantage of by predatory creditors and payday lenders or who find themselves in generational poverty and need help making changes. She knows there are nonprofits and church-related organizations that do this kind of work, but she wanted to help those most in need. A good listener who has always been passionate about helping others, Judy walks alongside the most vulnerable in our society, helping them feel hope and believe in themselves. Judy is still active in a congregation, but she sees her whole life as an opportunity to live out her Christian vocation.

■ Lindsay works with compromised children in a mental health facility. She went into nursing to help people, and she chose this job in particular because it allows her to make a human connection with frequently overlooked children. She understands the dehumanizing aspects of care provided in a pediatric acute mental health facility, even in necessary procedures and precautions. Lindsay takes special joy in advocating for people whose lives are filled with abuse and pain. She is passionate about making sure they have the care they need to take positive next steps on a long road toward wholeness.

Lindsay is involved in a congregation, but it is not a traditional kind of church. The child of a pastor, she developed a unique view on the extravagant waste of maintaining church buildings at the expense of helping hurting people. She is part of a faith community that intentionally has no building, so resources are spent to help those in need with whom the congregation seeks to develop relationships.

■ Daniel is an accountant with a major national firm who travels a lot on a rigorous work schedule. He spends his days identifying issues in corporations' financial systems and helping to ensure fair accounting practices. His work is important to him because he understands himself to be doing the right thing, the fair thing, on behalf of investors and employees of those corporations. Shaped by his upbringing in the church, Daniel now calls himself an agnostic but, in him, I saw a secular humanist who believes in the good that humanity can do. When asked where he sees good in the world, he describes the way his partner inspires him with her kindness, grace, and passion to help others through her work as a medical professional. Daniel is a man of few words: "She makes me better" is how he describes the good he experiences from his relationship with her. In this I hear the near sacramentality I heard in the relationships other study participants described with mentors and members of their congregations. Daniel's core beliefs are not inconsistent with the Christian faith of his younger years, but the incongruity of stated beliefs and lifestyle became too problematic for him. He lives his vocation with the support of family and a few close friends, driven by his passion for fairness and honor.

■ Simone is a special education teacher in a middle school in an affluent suburb. She chose her work because it allows her to advocate for children considered incapable of doing a variety of things. Using her voice on their behalf, she can help shape vocational and independent living options, plans that develop in middle school. Simone is intentional about advising the classroom teachers about the unique abilities of each child and suggests educational strategies to help each student work to his or her highest level.

Simone moved away from the church of her childhood as she struggled with its hypocrisy and authoritarian nature. The congregation of her adolescence helped exorcise some of her negative childhood experiences, but its current ministry just doesn't inspire her. She and her husband have considered reconnecting with a church, but she describes herself as being guided by her internal moral compass rather than by religious authorities.

■ As a child, Michelle found herself befriending the special education children in the inclusion classroom in her elementary school. It was something of a personal crusade of hers to stop other kids from being mean to them. As an adult, she was intrigued by why the world didn't seem to be working for some children. She recently completed a master's degree in early childhood special education and works as a classroom teacher in a nonprofit preschool with children who have developmental delays that are further complicated by their home situations. She describes feeling drawn to early childhood special education because it seemed to her that the greatest impact could be made early in these children's lives. A passionate commitment to sharing God's love plays a role in Michelle's investment in this work, although she is not presently active in a congregation.

Michelle talks about living her faith through her work in this way: "I know that today, for the 3.5 hours I had my kids [in school], they knew they were safe, had the food they needed, and there were people to give them hugs even if they were throwing sand or cussing. . . . That's a good day. Even on the worst days, there's something good."

Congregations are poorer when they shun questions young adults and youth ask, such as "Why do we need a building?" and "Why do we exclude folks who don't fit into our well-designed programs?" These questions can and should make settled congregations and their members uncomfortable. Questions like these certainly discomforted the religious leaders in Jesus' day when he asked them. And that's the point.

Congregations miss out on the enlivening presence and gifts of young adults and youth. They miss out on the resilient hope of those so committed to their vision that present circumstances cannot quench their passion. Congregations miss out on the wisdom and insight of those who see injustices and invest their lives in righting the wrongs.

I could go on to tell about other passionate twenty-somethings like Laurel, who provides doula services for clients regardless of their ability to pay; or Brandy, who uses her creativity through photography to tell the stories of the marginalized; or Marilyn, who often uses her own resources to care for humans and animals; or Sylvia and Pat, who live justly and mercifully with their neighbors in struggling neighborhoods of major cities just because it's the right thing to do, even though many don't return the favor. These young adults are not waiting for churches to create ministries through which they can volunteer. Instead, they are following their passions and giftedness to share God's love in practical and tangible ways, even if they don't explicitly use those words. In *Learning Mission, Living Mission*, Glynis LaBarre offers this insight:

> Christians in the missional movement choose to become actively involved in alliances with their community. They have discovered that acting on the truth of Christ's gospel makes a difference in the world. They form authentic relationships with others—Christian and non-Christian—while addressing

community problems. These efforts lead to true partnerships in which love, respect, and dialogue can arise as a natural part of working together.[4]

It can be easy to overlook the ministries of other people, such as young adults in fallow times, when they don't fit our expectations for church attendance and working through established programs. But people like the ones I interviewed live and work in neighborhoods all around our churches. Congregations can become healthier and more vital by opening their eyes to these passionate young (and not-so-young) adults who are living God's love in unexpected ways.

This is what I mean by "a faith to live for." Young adults and youth connect with the passion of the Christian faith, with the passionate teachings of Jesus. They sense this passion in ways that are often untempered by the kinds of life experiences that have boxed in or battered middle and older adults or that have anesthetized those grown-ups to the dreams that enlivened their younger years. Middle and older adults still need to be connected with their passions—to be reminded of them—and some, indeed, are. For those whose passions have waned, relationships across the age spectrum can be very important to reclaiming them. This brings us to the complex puzzle of being church across generations in the conclusion.

Notes

1. Carol Howard Merritt, *Tribal Church: Ministering to the Missing Generation* (Lanham, MD: Rowman & Littlefield, 2007), 5–6.

2. Adapted from *The Christian Citizen* © 2014. Used by permission of American Baptist Home Mission Societies. http://abhms.org/resources/christian_citizen/cc2014_1.cfm (accessed 3/25/2015).

3. Names and identifying information have been changed to protect interviewees' identities.

4. Glynis LaBarre, *Learning Mission, Living Mission* (Valley Forge, PA: Judson, 2012), 15.

Conclusion
Being Church across Generations

Back in chapter 1, we reflected on the meaning of adulthood. Scholars observe that being adult involves being aware that one is assembling a life and has agency in decisions about that life. Being adult means wrestling with an ongoing inner dialogue about truth and what is true, seeking to move closer to it. Being adult means responding to changing circumstances and reconstructing ourselves and our relationships with everything around us in light of those changing circumstances.[1] Being adult, I would reiterate, is not something a person completes, arbitrarily, as they reach age twenty-one or thirty or thirty-five. It isn't finished when a person reaches a particular relationship status like becoming a spouse or a parent. It isn't tied to vocational identity or socioeconomic bracket. This continual emergence into "grown-up-ness" which I have separated from the legal age of majority in our culture, is ongoing. Grown-ups continue to emerge throughout each stage and season of life. They need faith and faith community at each and every stage.

Because of the role of faith and communities of faith in making meaning, they are unique and useful tools throughout life. If frequent and sometimes massive change characterizes life early in adulthood, such changes often also describe older adulthood in even more permanent ways. Middle adulthood also carries the need to reconfigure and recompose our lives. Being adult means dealing with changing circumstances, realizing that we assemble and reassemble our lives as we wrestle with our truth and learn to relate to the world around us in new ways. Certain changes may be unwelcome, but they are normal and to be expected.

Agility and creativity in dealing with change are qualities and skills we continue to cultivate.

Remember Fern, who at ninety-six had lots of physical problems and personal issues about which she could have obsessed and in which she could have wallowed? That's tempting at her place in life when so much is going wrong or not working anymore and it feels too out of control. One way to survive all that, Fern illustrates, is to invest yourself and lift your eyes to a purpose larger than you. "Anything worth doing takes more than a generation."

In short, we need one another across the spectrum of life, because our lives are not so different in young adulthood from older or middle adulthood. As we grow older, perhaps we have come to know that we are more the same than different from each other all across the lifespan. We grow to learn how to treat other people. We come to understand about healthy boundaries and choosing our battles (and our words) carefully. We recognize that not everyone arrives at the same truth by the same path. So then why is it so difficult to remain connected across the age spectrum in the church?

Generational Theory Provides Insights

William Strauss and Neil Howe describe generations in congregations today using archetypal terms: "artist" (born 1925–42), "prophet" (born 1943–60), and "nomad" (born 1961–81). They describe the current emerging adults (born 1982–2002) as a "hero" generation. Although their specific findings about each generation are beyond the scope of this book, one insight is particularly helpful. In a detailed and complicated description of each generation, their writing reminds us that each generation was formed by certain experiences as children, which has caused them to react in certain ways as young adults and to become particular kinds of middle adults; and eventually each generation will grow into older adults whose perspectives are profoundly shaped by the experiences of the rest of their lives.

For example, my grandmother used to save aluminum foil and wash ziplock bags to reuse because she was shaped by her experience in the Great Depression—practices I found laughable as a younger person. She had particular biases against financial risk as an older person because of how she was shaped as a younger person—and so did I, yet in stark contrast with hers. Such biases leave open the potential for conflict when it comes time for the church to make financial decisions.

For those of us who live our beliefs in the context of the local church, a rich diversity of generations is a great gift but also a complicated reality. We recognize that all these generations of people are called to share leadership and journey together in the same congregation. However, all these different people hold all the different triggers and biases they have collected over the years so deeply that those biases are nearly invisible, even to the person holding them. It's almost as if we are sometimes blind to our biases without a "cane" to guide us as we journey together, bumping into each other over issues and not even fully understanding why.[2]

This business of sharing God's big tent of the church with other generations can feel nearly impossible at times. It is very difficult, but it can also be very rich. The hard work of paying attention to others on the path is critical. To do so requires that we grant others the abundant mercy and grace we ourselves also need.

Holy Listening

I came to this project with hunches about what interviewees would tell me had been important in their teenage lives as they look back now that they are young adults. I expected to hear about mentors and models—important people in their lives as teenagers whom they looked to for models of faithfulness. I half-expected to hear about people they saw as "Christian superheroes"—people they thought were nearly impossible to emulate, like their favorite pastors and youth leaders, college chaplains, and camp counselors.

I imagined I would find that service opportunities and mission trips would be important markers in the lives of youth as they became openings to discovering vocation and living out one's faith in ways that engaged passion. I expected to hear that youth group was more important to them than other ways they connected with the congregation. I thought I might hear about times when youth served as liturgists or vacation Bible school teachers or on church committees. I thought I might hear about involvements that call upon youth to give their gifts for the good of the whole or opportunities to find their own voices in communities of adults.

I further expected to find that those adolescents chose congregations in their young adulthood with what I had come to think of as a "more adequate theology" to assist them in dealing with the complexities of life. Indeed, I have listened to youth over the years as they wrestled with their church's teachings, often delivered via well-intentioned but clueless Sunday school teachers and other adults. They have struggled when they were told that God made that boy in their class at school have cancer to test his faith and that of his family. They have wrestled mightily with teaching like "God took Aunt Mable 'home,'" and that it was for the best because she was happier now. I often found youth attributing their agnosticism or atheism to the fact that they just couldn't believe God would do those kinds of things. Honestly, I have found myself agreeing that kind of God isn't one I can believe in either. I have observed that, as my own theology grew more complex, with fewer answers and more room for questions, my commitment to living my faith became deeper. In my interviews, I expected to find others for whom this happened. I thought I would find that these people as youth wanted a more adequate theology, and maybe they did, but that's not what they told me.

I confess that I came to this study with an investment in its findings. As one who has been in ministry with youth for more than two decades, I am deeply invested in understanding the stories and insights of these young adults. My hope through this work was to listen deeply and carefully to the stories and the meanings they conveyed. I wanted to appreciate the individuals and their journeys, as well as hear what their individual and collective voices might be saying to me as a researcher and practitioner. So I was open to having my hunches challenged or replaced with truer images and experiences.

A Word about Surprises

I readily admit that I was surprised by some of what I heard in participant responses to research questions in this study. While their responses confirmed some of my hunches, I mostly did not hear what I expected to hear. I expected them to tell me about things I thought might have been important to them in their adolescent years, which simply were not as important as I thought they might have been. For example, I expected to hear them talk about key mentors who made all the difference for them in their continuing involvement with the church. I did hear about mentors, but I also heard about faithful grown-ups whose names young adults couldn't even remember but who had supported them and made sure they had what they needed for youth mission trips and so on. That surprised me.

I thought I would hear more about big experiences—mission trips and national youth gatherings that deeply impacted these youth, and I did hear about those. I thought I would hear study participants describe the importance of finding a theology that more adequately reflected their experience of God in their lives, and I heard about that too. But I also heard about the impact of serving alongside grown-ups in a congregation in the midst of the day-to-day of regular church life, having their gifts valued or at least coming to realize there was something they could do that had an actual impact on people in need. I heard about the deep impact of living alongside faithful grown-ups who were living their faith tangibly. It was really not all about theology or big experiences, nor was it all about key mentors. That surprised me.

Perhaps what surprised me most, although I guess it should not have, was the holiness and depth of these young adults' times away from active congregational life. These seemingly fallow times were profoundly fruit-ful in healing, growth, and reflection. I was surprised to learn about the depth of what was going on inside during these times. And I was sur-prised by how much it mattered that there were people in their adoles-cent congregations who kept in touch during these times, in effect "teth-ering" them to the faith community during a time away. I say this should not surprise me, because I have found myself in that tethering role with grown-up youth from past youth groups. In holy moments of reflection over coffee or chats on Facebook, I have been present with young adults, doing what friends do.

If I distill all these surprises to their core, what I found through this project is actually an incredibly simple and straightforward prescription for the church. That prescription is something like *"Be* the church." And for each member of a congregation, "Be the best follower of Jesus you can be." Just do what God made you to do. Pay attention. Just *be* the church.

Perhaps what was most striking to me about the young adults I inter-viewed was the resilience I observed, the resilience of their hope in God—and sometimes resilience in the face of the church's failures. As I listened to young men and women describe growing up in the church, I heard stories of hope in the midst of struggle and love in the midst of trouble and pain. Their stories reminded me of the biblical stories I have heard throughout my life, telling of the people of God contending in relationship with their God in the Hebrew Scriptures: through the Exodus and the wilderness wandering, the glory days of the kings, the Exile. I hear genuine people complaining to and arguing with God, and an earthy God who gets fed up with them and some-times does regrettable things. I see the way the people learn from the experiences and grow in the ways they relate to God and understand themselves because they are entangled in love with one another and with God.

In young adults' stories of resilience, I heard echoes of the resilience of Jesus as he pressed on with his mission and ministry in spite of the resistance he faced from the temple officials, from people he grew up with in his hometown, and even from his own mother and siblings. I find it far more remarkable that Jesus was able to persist in living out his vocation than that he eventually died because of what he believed and enacted. Again and again, I saw Jesus' passionate engagement with life replicated in the lives of those I interviewed. More than looking for something "to die for," I saw study participants who were living faithful lives to the full. They were looking for something "to live for." It is interesting to observe that young adults weren't explicit or reflective about the role of Jesus in their lives. This perhaps bears further consideration.

Hearing the stories of the young adults I interviewed reminded me of Dori Grinenko Baker's image in the introduction of *Greenhouses of Hope*, where she tells of a community project to reclaim some run-down greenhouses near her home in Virginia. In the process of renovation, some greenhouses again house thriving and well-kept gardens. She describes noticing how, even in the unrenovated greenhouses, beautiful roses could be seen growing out of broken windows and through the partial roof, without the benefit of regular watering, fertilizing, or tending. Likewise, in many cases, even when they were not receiving the nutrients they needed from their congregations, study participants describe removing artificial boundaries and seeking nourishment for growth in faith outside the sometimes failed structures that meant to nurture them.[3]

The resilience of the young adults with whom I spoke reminded me of the emancipatory hope that Evelyn Parker contrasts with wishful thinking in her book *Trouble Don't Last Always*. Not content merely to stand by while they see injustice, sometimes even at the hands of the church itself, young adults today seem to expect "deliverance from . . . oppression through the power of God," which compels them to live, each in his or her own way, as "agents of change for God's justice."[4]

Their stories also reminded me of the hope and resilience in my own faith journey, despite shallow and confining theology, bumbling grown-ups, and the slamming of doors of possibilities. The kind of hope and resilience I heard backgrounded in the stories these young adults told about their adolescent experience in the church moved me deeply. I realize that's a confession more than a research finding, and I offer it to indicate the holiness of listening as these study participants reflected on their experiences in my presence.

When I embarked on this project to discover how the church could reclaim faith in and with so-called missing generations, I wanted to focus on those young adults who were deeply engaged in their congregations as adolescents—and who sustained (or regained) connections with a faith community in young adulthood. I believed it was in partnership with such young adults who were already committed to living out their vocations through the church that I would be most likely to hear the thick, rich descriptions which would, through careful analysis, offer the most useful insights into my questions.

In this book, I have sought to share what I have learned with you: to give voice to those young adults who found their way "back home" into active congregational life as adults. It has been my profound joy to journey with them. And it is my deepest hope that congregations might catch a glimmer of something through their stories that provides the impetus to turn around in their habits and practices to create safe spaces—even incubators—for young adults' passionate engagement in the gospel of justice and love.[5]

A song by Graham Nash titled "Teach Your Children Well"[6] offers insight into a final important reality about being church across generations. Nash's song is, for me, a piece of wisdom I chose to "go back and get" for myself, *sankofa* style, from my own elders. Although I will not quote them here, I commend the lyrics to you as poetically insightful. Google them for yourself. In the song, I hear Nash describing the ways each of us is formed by our relationships with each other. I hear a compelling call for relationship across generations, even though sometimes it's complicated and painful. The African concept of *ubuntu* sums it up best for me: *I am because we are.*

Notes

1. Sharon Parks, *The Critical Years: The Young Adult Search for a Faith to Live By* (New York: Harper & Row, 1986), 6.

2. William Strauss and Neil Howe, *The Fourth Turning: An American Prophecy* (New York: Broadway, 1997), 84. See also William Strauss and Neil Howe, *Millennials Rising: The Next Great Generation* (New York: Vintage, 2002).

3. Dori Grinenko Baker, ed., *Greenhouses of Hope: Congregations Growing Young Leaders Who Will Change the World* (Herndon, VA: Alban Institute, 2010), 9–11.

4. Evelyn Parker, *Trouble Don't Last Always: Emancipatory Hope among African-American Adolescents* (Cleveland, OH: Pilgrim, 2003), 15–16.

5. The Forum for Theological Exploration engages many of the same issues and questions as this study. For a wealth of resources, consult their website: www.fteleaders.org.

6. Graham Nash, "Teach Your Children Well," *4 Way Street*, recorded by Crosby, Stills, Nash, and Young, Nash Notes, 2002.

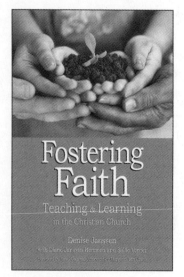